P9-EEI-101

Held in the Light

Held in the Light

Norman Morrison's Sacrifice for Peace and His Family's Journey of Healing

ANNE MORRISON WELSH

WITH JOYCE HOLLYDAY

ORBIS BOOKS

Maryknoll, New York 10545

I rejoiced when I heard them announce,
"The time of warfare is past.
No more will brother hate brother
or violence have its way.
No more will they drown out God's silence
and shut their hearts to his song."

Pray for peace in the cities
and harmony among the races.
May peace come to live on our streets
and justice within our walls.
With all my heart I will pray
that peace comes to live among us.
For the sake of all earth's people,
I will do my utmost for peace. (Psalm 122)
—STEPHEN MITCHELL,
A BOOK OF PSALMS

Contents

Acknowledgments

This book would not have been written had it not been for the encouragement my family and I received from hundreds of people both here and abroad after Norman Morrison gave his life to stop a war. Without such an outpouring of love and support, it would have been incredibly harder for me to deal with my husband's death and our loss. To all who reached out to us, my deepest gratitude. You held us in the Light.

There was also a smaller circle of Light surrounding and holding us up—friends, neighbors, and members of Stony Run Friends Meeting in Baltimore. I want to express special thanks to these dear Friends: Nancy and Herb Clark, Peggy and Allan Brick, Catherine Taylor, Henry and Mary Cushing Niles, Kitty Connor, Bob and Susie Fetter, Kathy Abt, Hooper and Molly Bond, Mary and John Roemer, Sam Legg, and George and Eleanor Webb.

There were other old friends from afar who stood by us in our work of healing, including Lillie Blanche Van Hoy, Bill Beidler, the Hoarty family, Lucy Christopher, Al Rabil, Bob Sigmon, Bob Hull, and Donald Reiman.

Over time, Hugh Ogden, Dorothy Mock, Beth and Mel Keiser, Judith Harvey, Elizabeth Kirk, Christian Appy, Penelope Bond, and Lady Borton encouraged me to tell our story—not only Norman's story, but also that of our family. This book is in part the result of your urging.

Because of the persistence of Bob Hull, Norman's Wooster classmate, and the invaluable assistance of Lady Borton and her staff at the Quaker Service office in Hanoi, we became intimately aware of a wider circle of new friends. To the many Vietnamese who opened their hearts to us, treating us like long-lost family, our thanks and tears are insufficient. We love you. We will never forget you and your beautiful land.

Through sharing our story at a Holy Ground retreat near Asheville, North Carolina, I met Joyce Hollyday, a gifted writer who took on the difficult job of editing and transforming my lengthy manuscript into this memoir. For her talent, dedication, and incredible patience, I offer gratitude and praise. And to John Talbot, of Talbot Fortune Agency, my appreciation.

Heartfelt thanks to Pendle Hill for nurturing my writing and for publishing our story in "Fire of the Heart," a Pendle Hill Pamphlet.

Thanks also to the American Friends Service Committee for opening for me valuable opportunities to work for peace and justice.

How fortunate we were to discover a knowing, patient, and sensitive compadre in Robert Ellsberg and Orbis Books—in so many ways a perfect fit.

Most of all, I am grateful for the love and respect unfailingly provided by my father and mother, William Howard Corpening and Mary Frances Marshall Corpening; for the rock-solid love and witness of Norman; and for the love and support of our children, Ben, Christina, and Emily, as well as David and Jonathan Welsh. To you all I will forever be grateful. Indelibly you are on every page of this book.

And finally, to Bob Welsh, my husband and partner of thirty-five years, who has quietly supported and lived with me through several lifetimes, my abiding love.

Introduction

To Shine a Light

*The life is mightier than the book
that reports it. The most important
thing in the world is that our faith
becomes living experience
and deed of life.*
—NORMAN MORRISON, FROM NOTES
WRITTEN ON THE DAY OF HIS DEATH

*F*or at least two decades, this book has been asking to be written. Maybe it was asking even earlier, as early as the days and weeks after Norman's death. Perhaps I knew I would write it some day, as I methodically collected news clippings, letters, and other mementos of November 2, 1965, carefully placing them in cardboard boxes. I hauled those boxes around for years, from one house to another, from one life to another, afraid to glance inside. For a long time, looking back was too painful.

As the years unfolded, I wrote pieces of this story, as did others affected by it. But only pieces, not the whole. Even this book is not the whole of Norman Robert Morrison's story. But it is the best that I can do, as his friend, his widow, and the mother of his children, left behind when he gave his life at the Pentagon in the hope of ending a terrible war. I offer the story with this disclaimer from Barry Lopez, who wrote in his book *Resistance:* "It is a sobering truth that only with the greatest difficulty can we convey our life, our meaning, to other people. Some essence always seems to evaporate with the translation into language."

Because the question has been raised, I want to say at the outset that I know that Norman Morrison was not insane that day, although he did what appeared to some to be an act of temporary insanity. I want to say, too, that I do not believe that he was a saint, though some people here and many in Vietnam considered him such. I think the deepest truth about Norman is that he was a person who cared—deeply, passionately, and finally desperately—about the things he believed in: peace and nonviolence, human rights, and an equitable sharing of the world's resources.

We were a young married couple during the turbulent 1960s, a decade of social ferment and change in America. We attempted, imperfectly but with devoted love, to raise a family in the midst of our involvement in that great turbulence. As Quakers, pacifists, and followers of Jesus, we watched with growing concern as a war escalated in a tiny country in Southeast Asia, on the other side of the globe. So much of what our country was doing in Vietnam felt deeply wrong to us.

As the horror of the war grew, it finally overwhelmed Norman. He was searching for a powerful and persuasive way to say no. Albert Camus once wrote, "In the midst of winter, I found there was, within me, an invincible summer." Camus' metaphor speaks to the yes that was hidden within Norman's no. This book is my attempt to share some of the yes of Norman.

Writing it is also an act of finding my own yes after his death, of sharing the challenging but blessed life that that indescribable loss decades ago presented to me and to our children. Though I was aware of the Quaker injunction to "let your life speak," I was totally unprepared for this kind of witness. After Norman's sacrifice, I felt as if a steel curtain dropped upon our home and our hearts. Then slowly, gradually, shafts of light appeared through that dark curtain, shining more and more brightly.

I found many reasons to go on living, devoting myself to our three children and to the cause of peace. I learned that pain and challenge hold the possibility of growth. I was given the strength to go on by the grace of God and the support of close friends and countless others, both seen and unseen. For a while, letters of encouragement arrived daily. Prayers and poems, too. They gave me energy and perspective—and a sense of purpose.

But my frozen grief would take years to thaw. From time to time, I attempted to peek into those boxes of memorabilia. But each time I opened one and took out an item, I would quickly put it back and close the box. Finally, one day I was able to read a letter. And then another. By some internal, eternal clock, it was time. Time to face my past and address the old aches in my heart. Little by little, I began to be healed. And I knew I was ready to share this story, with whoever wants to hear it.

In 1999, my family and I made an unforgettable journey to Vietnam. That trip opened our eyes and hearts to the depth of feeling the Vietnamese people of the war generation had, and still have, for Norman. Their story is also part of this story, a reminder that we all live in one world, that we are all interconnected. We are part of a larger picture, a mosaic that we alone cannot create, but to which each of us contributes an indispensable piece.

This is also a story about mystery—the mystery and awe of unexpected consequences. How one act or a single moment in one's life can set into motion so much, can affect so many—not only in the moment, but on throughout generations. Over time, countless unforeseen effects of Norman's sacrifice have emerged, as a fallen leaf floats out on the water, gets swept into a current, and goes far downstream. These mysteries, I believe, are part of what connects us to the heart of God and to one another.

Perhaps this is ultimately a story about healing—about how we get through our grief, doubts, and pain. Facing our deepest suffering and accepting what has happened to us is the beginning of healing. I learned the blessed necessity of accepting the irreversible past and forgiving both others and myself.

As I write these words now, more than four decades after Norman's death, our nation is mired in another war. Once again, reports from the other side of the globe inundate our senses with images of relentless suffering: air strikes and house-to-house searches, insurgent suicide bombings and improvised explosive devices, torture and mayhem. Once again, civilians of another nation are enduring devastation and displacement, body bags are coming home to the United States, and surviving soldiers are returning mentally traumatized and physically maimed. Once again, billions of our dollars are being siphoned off into war-making, while our schools, bridges, and hospitals deteriorate for lack of resources. If history is any indication, another war will follow this one, raining destruction on still another nation caught in the cross hairs of U.S. excess and control.

We human beings must find another way to address our differences and resolve our problems. I believe that Norman Morrison lit a fire and gave himself away in order to shine a light for the rest of us. To make it impossible for us to close our eyes or avert them from the hard truths of war. To show us a different path.

1

"What Can We Do That We Haven't Done?"

*Without the inspired act, no
generation resumes
the search for love.*
—NORMAN MORRISON

*T*he clock read just shy of 5:30, but already darkness was seep-
ing into the raw, early November day. Six-year-old Ben and five-
year-old Tina played nearby, while I put the finishing touches on
dinner. I wasn't worried, just wondering about the whereabouts
of Norman and our youngest child, Emily. Maybe they were at the
Taylor Home? As the executive secretary of Baltimore's Stony Run
Friends Meeting, Norman made frequent visits to the nursing
home the meeting sponsored. The residents of the home loved to
see children, and Norman often took Tina with him. Perhaps he
had taken Emily this time.

But it wasn't like Norman to be gone after dark. Maybe he had
been surprised by the early encroachment of night, as we had been
caught two days before by the shift away from daylight savings
time. We had forgotten to turn back our clocks and arrived at an
empty meetinghouse an hour early for our weekly Quaker meeting on Sunday morning. Norman suggested that we take a drive
out of the city and find a place to walk. Norman carried Emily,
almost a year old, on his shoulders. Ben and Tina darted ahead,
delighted to be "hiking" in their Sunday clothes. That dear image
of us all walking and laughing is the last family memory I hold in
my heart.

1

The phone in the hallway rang just after 5:30.

"Is this Mrs. Morrison?" an unfamiliar male voice asked.

"Yes."

"Are you the wife of Norman Morrison?"

"Yes."

For a moment, there was silence on the other end. Then the man identified himself as a reporter from *Newsweek* magazine. "Did you know that something has happened with your husband in Washington?" he asked. "I think it was a form of protest."

After a long pause, I mustered a "no." I felt as if everything inside my body stopped. I couldn't get my breath. The reporter became silent too, unable to say more. Immediately an image came to me of Norman, with Emily in his arms, wading into the Potomac River.

That surprising image was a picture of terror for me, connected to an old memory of watching my mother almost drown when I was four years old. We were in south Georgia. My family was at a picnic, surrounded by other families. Mother was swimming in the river, and I was sitting happily with my father on a blanket on the bank nearby. Suddenly Mother began screaming and waving her arms for help. Dad threw off his shoes and charged down the bank and into the water. Other men ran and helped him pull Mother out. Thankfully, she was OK, but my fear that I would lose her forever to the river stayed frozen in my memory. Now, all I knew was that something terrible had happened to Norman—and perhaps to Emily, too.

The reporter composed himself and interrupted the alarming thoughts that were overtaking me. "I think you'd better call the Fort Myer infirmary," he said gently. More than four decades later, I remain grateful for his merciful sensitivity, for not telling me what he knew and pressing to be the first to get my response. I wish now that I had taken note of his name.

Before I could focus on placing a call, the phone rang again. Another unfamiliar male voice was on the line. The man from the infirmary at Fort Myer, a military base near the Pentagon, informed me that Norman had been badly burned. He didn't tell me—and I didn't ask—if Norman had died. Intuitively, I knew that he hadn't survived. I asked the stranger on the phone if Emily was all right. He said that she was fine. "I'll be there as soon as I can," I managed to say, feeling as though the blood was draining out of me.

With trembling hands, I dialed the number of George and Eleanor Webb, close friends who were members of the Stony Run Friends Meeting. They were at our home within five minutes. I was still standing by the phone, paralyzed with shock. Eleanor gave Ben and Tina the supper I had made and what comfort she could. George and Harry Scott, another leader in the meeting who had arrived to help, insisted on driving me to Fort Myer.

I remember putting on my coat and walking out of the house with them. I had a sensation of being in a time warp—a moment so extraordinary that it is out of sync with real time—and then of walking off a gangplank. I didn't think about what I was going to do next. I just left our home and walked into another world.

On the drive to Washington, I sat in the back of the car, stunned and frozen, not knowing what to think or feel. None of us knew what to say. I stared out the window, mesmerized by the car lights playing on the darkness of the road. I recalled that Norman and I had been awed and moved by Buddhist monks in Vietnam who had protested through self-immolation. We had noted a small item in the newspaper in the spring about a Quaker woman in Detroit who had set herself on fire to protest the war. But these weren't events we had talked about at any length.

I remember having the thought that if Norman had tried to immolate himself, he would have succeeded. Though he was often unsure of himself when relating to people, and conversation didn't come easily to him, he was very confident with his hands; physical tasks were his strength. If he felt he had to do something, he would have found a way to do it.

I had no idea how to prepare myself for facing Norman's death. Or—if my intuition was wrong—for finding him severely burned to the point that he had been disfigured. I knew that he would have found that intolerable. So I prayed. I prayed for Norman. I prayed that his sacrifice would not be in vain. And I prayed for strength.

I retraced the details of our day together in my mind, searching for clues. Norman had woken up with a cold, so I drove Ben and Tina to school that morning. He stayed in bed most of the day, working on a New Testament class that he was to present to the meeting during the coming week. Emily played on the floor near us in our bedroom, until I put her down for her nap.

About noon I went downstairs and started to prepare lunch— French onion soup and grilled cheese sandwiches. Norman came down and perched on a stool on the other side of our big kitchen, talking about the Vietnam War, which we did regularly in those days. He mentioned an article he had just read about the bombing and napalming of a village by U.S. forces. He was particularly agonized by the suffering of the village's children.

"What can we do that we haven't done?" he asked. His tone was grave, but he didn't seem distraught or depressed. He appeared quite calm. I kept stirring the soup and then responded, "I really don't know." We had done everything I could imagine doing to try to stop the war: praying, protesting, lobbying, withholding war taxes, writing letters to newspapers and people in power. I remember adding, "All I know is that we mustn't despair."

We went into the dining room to eat our lunch, and the conversation moved to more pleasant topics. We talked about Christmas, about our plans to go to Erie, Pennsylvania, to be with his mother. He asked me what I wanted for a Christmas gift, and I told him that I would like a suit, something nice from a consignment shop. We went back upstairs and sat on the bed, glancing through the day's mail. Norman looked up at me and asked pensively, "What would you do if anything happened to me?"

"What a question!" I exclaimed. At first I wasn't sure whether to take him seriously or not. But after thinking about it for a moment, I said, "I guess I would take the children to Dad's, until I could figure things out." My father was living in Granite Falls, North Carolina, with my younger brother Bill. I had concocted the answer on the spot. I had never really contemplated not having Norman in our lives. Norman made no comment in response, and that was the end of that brief, puzzling exchange.

Emily was still asleep when I went to pick up Ben and Tina at school. Norman went back to preparing his class. He kept entirely to himself the mission he felt called to that day. If I had known what he was contemplating, I would have gone to any length on earth to stop him.

We were keeping a car—a very old, two-tone Cadillac—for our dear friends Harry and Mary Cushing Niles, while they were on a visit to India. When I got back home, the Cadillac was gone. I could not have imagined that Norman and Emily were at that moment on their way to the Pentagon. Or that our baby would be with her father right up to the fiery end of his life.

When George, Harry, and I got to the Fort Myer infirmary, we hurried in, pushing past the crowd of reporters that had gathered. The people who greeted us inside were very courteous. A man ushered me out of the lobby and into a small, private room, where he told me that Norman had died.

Soon a nurse came and handed me Emily, wrapped in a white blanket. She wasn't crying. She seemed serene and unaffected by the bright lights and strangers. Norman and I had faced the possibility of losing our youngest daughter even before she was born, and facing that risk again that day had seemed almost more than I could bear. I held Emily close, waves of relief flooding through me. After the nurse handed me her diaper bag, all I wanted to do was take her home.

Someone appeared with Norman's jacket, the Harris Tweed that we had bought in Scotland in 1957, right after we were married. It was his favorite. It symbolized his Scottish heritage, of which he was very proud. He loved to wear that coat. I remember thinking that it was right for him to want to die in his Harris Tweed. I was astonished, but somehow relieved, to see that it was only slightly singed.

Then I was handed Norman's wallet, comb, and wedding band. "Yes, these are his things," I confirmed to the infirmary officials, giving them the positive identification they needed. I remember thinking, "It's over. It's all over."

In the meantime, George and Harry had consulted. One of them said to me, "There are all kinds of media outside, and we probably should think about saying something." I knew they were right. "Yes, we should," I agreed.

We huddled in a corner. George had a spare envelope with him, and a pen. Heaven and my friends helped me to find the words to say. I spoke, and George wrote my words on the envelope. Then he went out and read my statement to the media: "Norman Morrison has given his life today to express his concern over the great loss of life and human suffering caused by the war in Vietnam. He was protesting our government's deep military involvement in this war. He felt that all citizens must speak their true convictions about our country's actions."

I'll never know exactly what happened outside the Pentagon during rush hour on November 2, 1965. Eyewitness reports conflict. What seems clear is that Norman—with Emily, her diaper bag, and a gallon-sized glass jug of kerosene in his arms—went to the river entrance of the Pentagon at dusk. He poured the kerosene over himself and struck a match on the top of one of his shoes.

A traffic policeman recalled seeing a man with a baby walking along the low parapet of a walled garden outside the Pentagon, and some onlookers claimed that Norman stood on that wall and shouted at the gathering crowd while he burned. Other witnesses reported that Norman and Emily were behind the wall, inside the raised rectangular garden laced with brick walks. A Pentagon guard who raced to an alarm box to call the fire department said the flames shot ten to twelve feet into the air.

At great personal risk, two military officers leapt over the wall and tried to smother the fire with their hands and coats, burning themselves in a futile effort to save Norman. He apparently fell forward then into a narrow trench and was trying to utter his last words, which none of the eyewitnesses could understand. A young doctor on duty at the Pentagon dispensary got a two-word summons: "Somebody burning." Norman was unconscious but still alive when the doctor got to him. He was gasping for breath, according to the doctor, and died a few minutes later in the ambulance, on the way to the infirmary.

Much later, a doctor told me that Norman probably died of suffocation rather than from burns. The fire consumed all the air around him. When a person dies this way, it happens very quickly. I was thankful for the mercy of that. I wanted desperately to believe that Norman hadn't suffered long.

In an office inside the Pentagon, an aide interrupted Robert McNamara, then Secretary of Defense, to tell him that something was happening outside. McNamara, who later declared that Norman had set himself on fire within forty feet of his third-floor window, saw the last of the flames and the two ambulances that had arrived. "It's what?" he asked the aide, according to one report, the color draining from his face when he saw paramedics bundling Norman's near-lifeless form. Another "What?" was all that McNamara could muster when the aide mentioned that there was also a child.

What of Emily? That remains the great mystery. Some eyewitnesses reported that Pentagon employees poured out of the building toward the pillar of fire, yelling to Norman, "Drop the baby!" and "Save the child!"—prompting him to throw Emily out of his arms. Others say Norman set her down, and still others that he handed her over to an unidentified woman in the crowd. The coroner's report stated that he dropped Emily, who landed unharmed in a bush.

What I believe is that Norman held our precious youngest child as long as he dared, then placed her on the ground and struck the match. What I know is that Emily, dressed in light-blue coveralls under the white blanket, had no cuts or bruises, no singes or burns, on her small body. She seemed miraculously calm and well when I gathered her into my arms at the infirmary. I held her as close as I could, as if I would never let her go. Then it was time for me to take her home and face a future I couldn't begin to imagine.

2

Relying on "Guided Drift"

*I dare not fail to respond to
guidance, for my whole life
depends upon it.*
—NORMAN MORRISON

*O*n the way home that night—and in the few quiet moments I was able to find in the days that followed—I pondered what kind of man Norman Morrison was, and what had driven him to sacrifice himself. We had found each other ten years earlier in a leafy glen at Chautauqua in the summer of 1955. A classmate from Duke University had invited me to this enchanting religious, educational, and recreational community in western New York state. Attracted by the promise of a summer filled with music, drama, and adventure, I boarded a train in North Carolina and made the long journey north.

A local bus dropped me off at Chautauqua's front gate. In awe, I carried my suitcase along its narrow streets and brick walks, passing rows of old, side-by-side Victorian houses. Unlike the southern homes with which I was familiar, these sat snug to the ground, looking self-contained, as if they had been there forever and knew all the secrets of the place. Trees arched over everything—the largest maples I'd ever seen, and beech and birch trees such as we did not have in the South.

I was employed to wait tables at Chautauqua's Cary Hotel. One Sunday evening, urged by curiosity, I attended a "glen service." I joined the gathering of young folks under a canopy of tall

8

trees, by a rocky stream that ran through a shallow ravine on the south end of the grounds. I enjoyed singing the hymns, and hearing scriptures read and prayers offered, around a campfire. But I was really there hoping to meet more fun-loving Chautauqua bell hops and bus boys with their '50s-era crew cuts.

It was a summer of religious questioning and soul-searching for me. At the time, I couldn't honestly say that I believed in God, much less Jesus Christ. But I did embrace a code of ethics, largely gleaned from the writings of Martin Buber and a small book by Daniel Saville Muzzey titled *Ethics as a Religion*. That's what I spoke about when I was invited one Sunday to lead the service.

As I was leaving the campfire that evening, a pleasant, earnest-looking young man caught up with me. He had a quick walk and a friendly smile, and he complimented me on my talk. We chatted easily as Norman walked me back to the Cary Hotel, though I must have been speaking rather loudly. As we passed a cluster of darkened houses nestled together, he gently grabbed my arm and said, "Shush, not so loud! The old folks are sleeping."

I was slightly offended by the reprimand, but nonetheless I agreed to accept his invitation to an opera. Something about this intense young man interested me. Maybe it was the twinkle in his blue-gray eyes. During the ten days that remained for me that summer at Chautauqua, Norman and I saw a great deal of each other.

Genetically, Norman was a "double Scot"—a McDonald on his mother's side and a Morrison on his father's. Norman was strongly grounded in, and proud of, his Scottish roots. Legend has it that Norman's Morrison ancestors were washed onto the rocky coast of northern Scotland from Norway. His family possessed the characteristics believed to be typical of the Scots-Irish folk who settled in the mountains: strong, independent, proud, fatalistic. People whose main challenge, according to one historian, was "to cultivate courage in the face of . . . cosmic uncertainties."

Norman was a fierce competitor. At the College of Wooster, his classmates dubbed him "the fighting Quaker"—for his behavior both on and off the intramural football field. He was also known as "Where-there-is-a-will-there-is-a-way Morrison." Though neither large nor unusually muscular, he was tough and fearless.

Norman tried many things, and succeeded at most of them. He loved canoeing, fishing, swimming, and skating. Though he was tone deaf and failed at every effort to learn a musical instrument, he was a great dancer, with a particular fondness for polkas. In high school he participated in the debating society and won awards for patriotic speeches. He was a leader in youth activities in his church and attained the rank of Eagle Scout, receiving the God and Country award.

Norman's family bought a cottage at Chautauqua in the mid-1940s, and his summers there had a deep impact on him. Mabel Powers, a devotee of Native American lore, likely was his first role model of a peacemaker. She taught about the confederation created by the Six Nations of the Iroquois, conducting a peace council when Norman was eight years old in the same ravine where he and I met thirteen years later. She talked about the power of fire, both physical fire and the fire of love and courage that burned inside each of the young people who were listening.

Charles Hagadorn, a beloved pastor, introduced Norman to the idea of listening to God and to the social and political impact of faith in the world, playing a role in Norman's deciding in high school to enter the Presbyterian ministry. And Marguerite Smith, a history teacher, was a liberal thinker and adventurous free spirit who challenged Norman's mind. While Norman was in her class, she contracted a crippling disease that over time paralyzed her body—but not her mind—and through the years Norman always stopped by to "talk politics" at her bedside. Ironically, though she was seriously ill, she outlived her former student.

Norman's mother, Hazel Fuller Morrison, worked as a secretary for a paper company and was gentle, conscientious, and shy. His father, Stanley Failes Morrison, whom friends and family affectionately called "Doc," was a highly successful dentist in

Erie, Pennsylvania. He was strong, witty, willful, and quick to anger, with high expectations for Norman and his younger brother, Ralph. Though Norman excelled in many things, he always seemed to fall short in athletics and academics, the endeavors that most would have satisfied his father. In his early years, Norman seemed to have spent much of his energy either trying to find ways to please his father or to stay out of his way, and he believed himself to be a deep disappointment to him—a burden I suspect Norman bore to the end.

Norman's father suffered from recurring bouts with ulcers. Toward the end of 1946, he spent several weeks in Florida recuperating, missing Christmas with his family and an emergency appendectomy Norman underwent. He died, quite unexpectedly and rather mysteriously—the official cause of death was recorded as "internal hemorrhaging"—on January 28, 1947, soon after Norman's thirteenth birthday. During that time, Norman began keeping a diary, a habit he continued for the rest of his life. He also began reading the Bible, which he did "each and every evening until March 22, 1949," he recorded in his diary, "when I finished every word of the King James version."

On a warm August evening, just days before I would leave for home, Norman "borrowed" the old laundry truck he used to make deliveries on the Chautauqua grounds and drove me to Corry, Pennsylvania, where his mother's people had a family farm. Corry, which had been the home of Norman's great-aunt Margaret and great-uncle George, was a safe haven from family stresses, the place where, as a young boy, Norman had gone again and again for love and comfort. It was where he learned about the land, making horsetail tea, pulling rhubarb, and picking apples under the tutelage of Margaret, whom he called "Auntie," though she was more like a mother to him. By the time he was seventeen, Norman was working five acres of the Corry property himself—digging a well and basement for a house, planting fruit seedlings and flowers, developing a dream.

As we bumped along through the countryside in the old laundry truck that August evening, chatting away, I kept studying

Norman, wondering about the source of his intensity. Little did I know that my visit to Corry was a kind of initiation. Corry was Norman's retreat and the home of his heart. I had to like Corry.

We stopped first at the old McDonald farmhouse. Uncle George had long since died, and Aunt Margaret was in a nursing home. Norman had befriended the family who owned the place by then. The owner allowed us to wander through the old, dark house and around the yard and barns.

Next door was Norman's five acres. It was easy to admire the obvious hard work he had devoted to his land. The fruit trees he had planted were thriving. One of the older trees was ripe with summer apples. I began picking some of them off the ground when suddenly many more started falling. I looked up and saw Norman in the tree, shaking down the apples with a mischievous grin. "Give me a warning next time you do such a thing!" I yelled up at him.

Later that evening, some of our Chautauqua friends joined us for a corn roast. Norm built a big fire. When it had settled down into hot coals, he placed a large sheet of tin over it, and on top of the tin laid dozens of fresh ears of corn, wet in their husks. Never before had I eaten corn prepared that way, so delicious.

I guess I passed the Corry test. Norm didn't say anything to me then, but years later I found this terse entry in his diary: "Anne and the farm wonderful." The farm was indeed wonderful. Yet I didn't feel at home there. Was there something lonely and sad about the place? A little too isolated? Could I imagine myself in the house that might some day rise out of the little excavation Norman had started? If so, what would I/we do in a house on a hill above a small town in the "icebox" of Pennsylvania?

I was born in the deep South, in Valdosta, Georgia, on what is known as Juneteenth Day. On June 19, 1865, Union troops rode into Galveston, Texas, to enforce the Emancipation Proclamation, which Abraham Lincoln had signed more than two years earlier. I was born on the seventieth anniversary of that day, in 1935. My father, William Howard Corpening, told me about it before I was old enough to understand, but I got the idea that my birthday had a special significance.

My mother, Mary Frances Marshall Corpening, was from an upper-middle-class family in Eufala, Alabama, a thriving landmark in the antebellum era. Dad was from a large farm family from the red-clay foothills of western North Carolina. Both were loving, kind, and generous. They shared care of the home, with Dad doing all the gardening and preserving of food and jams, and Mother most of the cooking and cleaning—except for washing the dishes, which Dad insisted he enjoyed. My father had an unusually egalitarian attitude toward women for that time. Perhaps he inherited this from his father, who sent his five oldest children, all girls, to college, while his four sons had to make their own way into higher education.

The home in which I grew up was a place where children were respected and appreciated. Dad, who made a living selling citrus-orchard sprays, was the family anchor and a great role model: calm, steady, easygoing, possessing inner strength and a cheerful outlook. After long summer days of playing tag and "Tarzan" in the vine-entangled woods behind our house, my older brother John and I would drowse lazily over our comic books after supper. With a slight twinkle in his water-blue eyes, Dad would say to Mother, "Babe, I think I'll do their feet tonight; it's hard for them to really get the dirt off their knees." Then, pipe between his teeth, he came quietly to where we were sitting, soap and towel in one hand and a basin in the other. He would spread a section of newspaper on the floor and then gently guide our feet into the warm water.

We lived comfortably in Valdosta when I was very young. I had an African American nanny named Louella Polite. When the Depression hit, Dad lost his job, and Louella was the first casualty. I remember feeling like the second. I had a great love for her, and losing her affected me deeply.

Because of my parents' progressive ideas and my special relationship with Louella, from a very young age I was sensitive to injustice and prejudice. I ignored my best instincts one day when

I joined in with a group of kids who were running and taunting an elderly black man walking nearby. After uttering rude words to him, I tripped and fell to the ground. The sand in my mouth seemed like certain punishment from the Almighty. I vowed never again to behave like that.

As a first-grader in rural Georgia, I wondered why the black children in the little house near us didn't attend our school just across the road. Many evenings I carried extra food from our table to theirs. In the second grade, I announced to Mother that I was having nothing more to do with Santa Claus, because he had given only an orange to my friend Jeanette. My parents were great admirers of Franklin Delano Roosevelt, and when I was about eleven years old, I was touched when my mother, using the common language of the day, said proudly that she thought I "would do something for the colored people some day, like Eleanor Roosevelt."

When Dad lost his job, we left Valdosta and moved to southwest Georgia, and then a few years later, to Union Grove, North Carolina, where Dad had accepted a position teaching high school vocational agriculture. He was a beloved teacher, affectionately nicknamed by his students "Old Scout." My father shocked those students by declaring, before the 1954 Supreme Court decision on desegregation, that he wouldn't mind at all if the school integrated and a black student sat next to his daughter. "I, for one," he announced, "am ready to integrate."

Our family attended the Union Grove Methodist Church. Often on Sunday mornings my grade-school friends and I would pick a few sweet shrub flowers, which we called "sweet buddies" or "sweet bubbies." If we had a handkerchief, we'd make a pouch for the deep wine-colored blossoms. If not, we'd hold them tightly in our palms, whose warm moisture released the flowers' sweet, heady fragrance. Sniffing it helped us endure many a tedious sermon on a hot summer day.

My brother John grew to be brilliant, high strung, and willful. Virtually expelled from the tenth grade, he had to go live with relatives in another county for the rest of that school year. In contrast, I became the quiet, helpful peacemaker of the family.

When I was fourteen, my brother Bill was born. I had been waiting all afternoon for Dad to come home from the hospital with the news. When I heard our Ford finally pull into the backyard, I was out the door in a flash. Opening the car door very deliberately, a trace of a smile on his face, Dad announced the birth of William Howard Corpening Jr.

As I hugged Dad in delight and relief, I felt his comfortable body sag a bit. Straightening up, he filled his pipe from the ever-present can of Prince Albert tobacco in his hip pocket, a ritual that preceded almost every conversation with him. "You see, Anne," he began stoically, "the baby's not quite right." My face fell. "The doctor told me that he could tell by the quality of his skin and the palms of his hands," he continued. "There's something wrong." When I asked what it was, Dad gave me a look of immense resignation and said, "I don't know. He's just not right."

When Bill was eighteen months old, a psychologist told my parents four things about their youngest child: he had Down syndrome; he would never be violent; he would probably be happier in his life than they would be in theirs; and he would live about thirty years. The psychologist was right on three of four counts. Bill quickly became our "Sweet Buddy" and has lived almost twice as long as predicted.

After seven memorable years in Union Grove, Dad lost his job again, and we moved to Granite Falls, North Carolina, where I graduated from high school in 1953. The next fall I entered Duke University, a wonderful choice and challenge for me. At Duke I was active in the Methodist Student Fellowship, under the tutelage of chaplain Art Brandenburg. But, like many young adults on their own for the first time, I began to question the faith of my youth.

In the midst of my wrestlings with disbelief, a teacher, Helen Bevington, opened the world of poetry to me. I hope I will never forget her radiant face as she recited the poems of Gerard Manley Hopkins, the nineteenth-century Jesuit cleric who wrote,

> *The world is charged with the grandeur of God.*
> *It will flame out, like shining from shook foil.*

Encountering those words and images, I felt an explosion of reverence and joy within me. Hopkins opened an exciting doorway of imaginative language for me, and his faith spoke powerfully to the understanding to which I was returning—a belief that, no matter the ills and shortcomings of the world, God and Christ are mercifully present.

One Sunday morning I walked into a former military hut on campus that was home to the Durham Society of Friends, or Quakers. When I entered the plain, narrow building for the first time, I saw a few people with heads bowed, sitting on folding chairs in a half circle around a pot-bellied stove. My first surprise was the plainness of the meeting room. The second was seeing my psychology professor, Donald Adams, whom I greatly admired, sitting there. He could not easily have seen me enter, but when he spoke, it was as if he spoke to me: "There is a God beyond the God of our theology and creeds. It is this God, this Ultimate Reality, we seek, and it is this whom we would worship." In the Great Silence that followed, I knew that my soul had found its home.

My father, who revered nature and believed in the general goodness of people, often said: "Life and the natural world are a great mystery. Isn't it wonderful that we cannot completely understand it!" Among the things I couldn't understand was my attraction to Norman Morrison. We were a study in contrasts in so many ways. But clearly something was being kindled between us in my final days at Chautauqua in the summer of 1955.

The spark took hold first within Norman. Just before I was to leave for home, we shared our last date that summer at a concert. When the music ended, we walked down to the bell tower by the lake. Waves were lapping against the large, gray rocks of the shoreline. We sat on a wooden bench under a huge willow tree.

Norman put his left arm around me, turning me so that I was facing him. His eyes danced, and he smiled a knowing smile. As for me, I was feeling a bit sad that Chautauqua was coming to an end. I gazed intently at Norman and saw a happy and attractive young man. His youthful face appeared guileless, and it conveyed determination and strong character. His thick, slightly wavy chestnut hair, broad forehead, and square jaw defined his face.

Unbeknown to me, Norman was holding his fraternity pin in his right hand. In an earnest voice, he explained that before he met me, he had had a clear plan for his life. After graduation, he was going to attend seminary, then take his middle year of graduate study in Scotland. There he would meet the girl of his dreams—"a Scottish lassie"—who would become his bride. I had thrown a monkey wrench into that plan.

"I hadn't planned on this, you see—on meeting you," he said. "I spent all last night awake, trying to decide what to do. Like Jacob, I wrestled with an angel. Over you. Over what to do." With that puzzling reference to the biblical character who prevailed in a nightlong wrestling match with a messenger of God, Norman handed me the fraternity pin.

I was stunned. But even as I took the pin and looked at it, murmuring some words of appreciation for the compliment, I protested, "I can't take this, Norm. We've had a lovely time together these past days, but still, we hardly know each other. No, I can't take it. I'm sorry." I spoke firmly. I tried to return the pin, but Norm made no move to accept it.

"Oh, but you see," he said calmly, the twinkle still in his eyes, "I can't take it back, because it's no longer mine. It doesn't belong to me anymore." For a long moment I was silent and perplexed, trying to figure out what to do next. "It's yours," Norm continued, "to do whatever you want with it. Hide it away, if you wish, in the bottom of a drawer. Put it in a shoebox. You don't have to wear it, you know."

I was unconvinced, but I had no immediate answer. I liked Norman. I found him strong and fascinating, even if a little quirky at times. But I had no intention of considering myself "pinned" to him. Being pinned was a prelude to engagement, I explained emphatically. Still, I couldn't think of what to do with the pin. It was clear that Norman wouldn't take it back, and I felt it would be rude to just leave it on the bench. I took the little pin back to my room and hid it in a corner of my suitcase. Eventually it ended up in the bottom of my dresser drawer at home.

Norman went back to the family cottage that night victorious, confiding to his diary that he had "pinned Anne Corpening. She couldn't believe my stubbornness, but confessed she liked it." On the following day, he reflected, "Men can sometimes pull a surprise on the fairer, stronger sex and get away with it."

On my way home from Chautauqua that summer, I thought over and over about the unusual and determined person I had met, and about the pin tucked away in a corner of my suitcase. I couldn't believe I had actually accepted it, though I had to admit that I was attracted to Norman. I might have preferred someone a little taller than an inch or two above my 5'9". Yet his open, Scottish face was pleasant and handsome. His smile was broad and sincere. He seemed utterly without pretense. His frame was spare, yet I was struck by the strength of his arms and the sureness of his hands. There seemed to be a knowing in his hands, an assurance about the things of the earth. That part of Norman reminded me of my father.

In the weeks that followed, Norman wrote to me nearly every day. Regarding the pin, he made the following comments in letters to me:

> 8/24/55: *Anne, I feel that I have come to a great mountain that I am anxious to climb. The reason I did what I did a week ago may be that I am desperately in need of someone who understands, to climb it with me or at least intelligently encourage the process. . . . Remember, there is*

no more true value than human relationships, unless it be a spiritual union.

9/12/55: All I can say is that I gave you the pin because I couldn't help giving it to you and I have every reason to believe that your taking it sprang from a mutual feeling.

9/21/55: As for the last night, it was as much a planning surprise for me as it was a momentary surprise for you. I never once really doubted that you would take the pin and yet I couldn't rationalize or explain my certainty.

His tussle with the angel is an example of what Norm often referred to as "guided drift." As I got to know him better, I became more familiar with his philosophy of guided drift, which was about being open to direction by God, staying in tune in case a message came from the Divine. Norm used to confess, "It is sometimes more drift than guide."

In the Quaker tradition, it is often called "holy obedience." In a Quaker meeting, where Friends wait prayerfully for God's guidance and inspiration, the worshiper's job is to listen, then try to respond. Norman believed that his life depended on responding faithfully.

Norman told me that when he was wrestling with the angel, he had received a vision of the union of our two lives. And thus began our long-distance, rocky ride—which survived, I am convinced, because God intended it. We were very different in temperament and family background, yet we loved each other and felt a sense of destiny about our relationship.

While Dad seemed to accept Norman from the beginning, Mother had a difficult time. As a Yankee, Norm was at polar opposite from Mother's upbringing and experience in the Old South. The first time Norman visited our home in Granite Falls, North Carolina, he had hitchhiked all night from Pittsburgh, where he was attending seminary. He always had great luck getting rides. He carefully dressed up in a sport coat and bow tie, carrying his suitcase with its big "W" from Wooster College on it. He thought it also helped that he had an open and honest face.

After his all-night journey, he phoned from the outskirts of Granite Falls, and I hastily drove out to the highway to pick him up. When we got back to the house, Mother offered to fix Norman some breakfast. He replied, somewhat abruptly, "I've had my apple." It was simply the truth, maybe a response from fatigue or pride, but Mother took it as a rebuff to her Southern hospitality, and the remark got the two of them off on the wrong footing. Norman soon excused himself and went upstairs to sleep for several hours—probably a smart move.

Mother simply didn't understand someone so thrifty and short of speech as Norm. And she still harbored grandiose dreams of the person her only daughter should marry—"someone like Eric Sevareid," she once suggested. Unfortunately, the disapproval was mutual. Norm didn't take to Mother, and he lacked the social graces or awareness to smooth the situation. And so it continued.

Even though I was fascinated with Norman, even though I loved him, I had recurring doubts as to whether we should marry. Some of those doubts related to Norman's attitude toward money, which was tight-fisted, but also to his eccentric streak, which surfaced unexpectedly from time to time. Nevertheless, on September 7, 1957, two years after meeting at Chautauqua, Norman and I were married in the new Durham, North Carolina, Friends Meetinghouse.

Although I sometimes wondered if I had married Norm against my better judgment, I am most assuredly glad that I did. We shared a love and a mutual outlook in faith, ideals, and vocation, all of which were important to me. And I just plain admired his grit and determination. We were like two practical mules hitching ourselves to a wagon, pulling together for some mission yet to be revealed.

Soon after our wedding, we left for study abroad at New College and the University of Edinburgh in Scotland. We were newlyweds in a cold basement flat living on love, the wonder of a foreign country, and a tight budget. Our only heat sources were a tiny coal grate in the living room and a small gas heater in the bedroom that had to be fed with shillings. For economy's sake, we rarely used the bedroom heater, and Norman was so cold he wore a stocking cap to bed. During studies, we sat in unheated classrooms in overcoats and hats, our gloves cut open at our fingertips so that we could take notes. My hands stayed cold from the day we arrived in late September until we left the following March.

We wanted a tree for our first Christmas together, but we didn't have the money for one. Some friends who lived on a large estate outside the city invited us to dinner one evening, and with their permission, we cut a few branches from a giant, curly yew on their property. We carried them home on a bus. Norman deftly bound them together with some wire into the shape of a tree, which we anchored in a pot on the buffet and decorated with ornaments sent by Norm's mother, Hazel.

That Christmas we got acquainted with English trifle and plum pudding. The university threw a party, complete with a Yule log and a boar's head with an apple stuck in its mouth, ceremoniously carried in on a platter by a group of singing Scots. We learned to eat haggis, the traditional Scottish dish made from unmentionable parts of sheep. Christmas carols both familiar and new to us were sung, much to our delight. On Christmas Day, Edinburgh was alive with bells. Scotland continued to enchant us, and we could have stayed there through the year had not the mysteries and wonders of the rest of Europe called to us by spring.

We traveled for six months, with Hazel joining us for a stretch in midsummer. It is to the credit of all three of us that we had only one squabble in six weeks of rather intimate travel. Norman was both embarrassed and incensed by the U.S. invasion of Lebanon that summer. We were in Rome when we heard the news, sharing a large room in a hostel. It was close to the Fourth of July, and Hazel wanted to celebrate and have some fun. "Don't you two get tired of worrying about politics?" she asked, lying on the bed and kicking up her heels in flamboyant disgust.

During our travels, Norman and I survived a turbulent crossing of the North Sea and a blizzard in the Austrian Alps. We reveled in the artistry of Greek architecture and the brilliance of spring flowers in Italy. All across Europe we found beauty and surprises.

We did not want to think of leaving this yearlong honeymoon, but the pull of our families persuaded us to return home in August 1958. Mother was battling cancer, and Norman's grandparents were failing. I guess it was an unconscious symbol of my reluctance to return that I wore the wool suit that I had on when I boarded the boat in England off and on during the entire voyage, until the August swelter won out as we neared our native shore. A day out, I changed into something sleeveless for the East Coast heat wave we were entering.

During our year abroad, our perceptions had been altered. New York City's East River docks looked appallingly dirty upon our return. My first impulse was to pick up all the paper I saw on the city's sidewalks. The waste and consumption that were generally part of the American way of life were hard for us to come home to. And I'm sure that we were hard for our friends to take. We were obnoxiously judgmental for at least a year after our return; it's a wonder we had any friends at all in Pittsburgh. Still, we were home.

I studied in the Graduate School of Child Development at the University of Pittsburgh, and Norman completed his degree at Western Theological Seminary (now Pittsburgh Seminary). In Edinburgh, Norman had found himself caught in a moral dilemma over ordination. He loved to preach and was good at it. But with growing conviction, he believed that the Presbyterian ritual of recognizing new ministers through the "laying on of hands" smacked of elitism, and he was increasingly drawn to the Quaker practice of the "priesthood of all believers." During our travels throughout Europe, we had visited several Quaker centers, learning about their work for peace and reconciliation, and this had made a strong impression on our hearts and minds.

Even before he graduated from seminary, Norman knew that his place was not in a Presbyterian pulpit.

Our decision to join the Pittsburgh Friends Meeting—and for Norman, casting his professional lot in that direction—was a spiritual homecoming for us. The Quaker traditions of pacifism and concern for world peace, justice, and equality resonated with my deepest inner promptings. The reverence and vitality of silent worship brought me deeply into God's presence.

It was a time of exciting spiritual and personal growth for us, blessed by a big event. On May 12, 1959—the day Norman graduated from seminary—our first child, Benjamin Howard, was born. I began to have labor pains the evening before at the baccalaureate service. The next day, a very happy Norman passed out cigars to his fellow graduates lined up for commencement.

In early summer, we moved to my parents' home in Granite Falls—our first step toward Charlotte, North Carolina, where we would work for two years to establish a Friends Meeting and Quaker outreach program. In September we packed Ben, our clothes, wedding gifts, a bassinet, and a playpen into our Volvo sedan and moved into the second floor of the meetinghouse in Charlotte, furnishing our living quarters with yard-sale purchases. Referring to a hurricane that struck that same month, Norman recorded in his diary, "Gracie and we hit Charlotte together. Nothing could have dampened our spirits with this new home."

Everything felt new and full of promise—a new job, a new location, and, most wonderful of all, a new baby. Our marriage was still new, as well, and it was exciting to be at the beginning of a great enterprise that we shared. There was entertaining to do, which we enjoyed immensely. I helped Norman with the Charlotte Friends Meeting newsletter and started a First Day (Sunday) school for children of the meeting.

We were both eager for this opportunity for service, and there was much that gave us joy. But as time went on, I began to see that the challenge was often daunting to Norman. Our sponsors, who were also our employers, were more theologically and politically conservative than we were. Tensions soon arose between Norman and officials of the North Carolina Yearly Meeting, which created stress within our Quaker group and our home. "Can't you be a bit more diplomatic?" I asked Norm when he returned home from a Yearly Meeting session, exasperated over an argument about the virgin birth. "You don't always have to be *that* honest about your beliefs."

Norman was greatly committed to peace and social justice and worked hard for these goals. Our new meeting frequently sponsored public discussions on political issues. We brought to Charlotte a controversial traveling docudrama from the American Friends Service Committee called *Which Way the Wind?* The *Charlotte Observer* arts editor called it "a Quaker search for alternatives to world suicide with hydrogen bombs." The reviewer said the play—which quoted philosophers, authors, and politicians, all toward proving that only love can conquer hate, and that evil never results in good—"left a lot of people wondering and worrying" in the packed auditorium.

Our second year in Charlotte was particularly full and difficult. Tensions continued between Norman and the Yearly Meeting. In May, we discovered that my mother's cancer had spread throughout her bones, which her doctor described as "like a sieve." When Dad gave me the news, I felt as though the bottom were dropping out of my life.

But October 24 brought another joyful arrival. After a long and difficult labor, Anna Christina was born. Tina, as we called her, was pure delight, with expressive eyes and a rosebud mouth that gave her a resemblance to a beautiful kewpie doll. I was thrilled to have a daughter, though she seemed so feminine to me that I wondered how I, who had been such a tomboy in my youth, would be able to raise her properly.

After Tina's birth, Norm and Ben grew particularly close, sharing a variety of gardening and other outdoor projects. Ben, who was an exceptionally strong little boy, loved being with his father. In just a few months, Tina was watching Ben's every move with delight.

Early in 1961, the civil rights movement came to Charlotte. It had spread from nearby Greensboro, where four students at North Carolina Agricultural and Technical University had sat in at the Woolworth's lunch counter, launching the student sit-in movement. Norman didn't hesitate to join an effort to desegregate a downtown theater, which was covered on national TV news. Hazel called from Pennsylvania that evening, her gentle voice betraying a touch of anxiety. "Was Norman involved in a demonstration at a theater in Charlotte?" she wondered. When I asked how she recognized him, she replied, "I would recognize the back of his head anywhere." Norm's action prompted some mean-spirited, anonymous phone calls to the meetinghouse. Norm's comment in his diary about it all was characteristically taciturn: "Stood with Negroes at Carolina Theatre. Got on TV for it."

In the spring, Mother became too weak to leave her bed. Twice a week, I put Tina in her little infant recliner seat and drove with her to Granite Falls. She was good medicine for her grandmother's soul, and for mine as well. Mother was eventually hospitalized and slipped into a coma, then roused one day and told me about a dream she had of flying in an airplane (which, to my knowledge, she had never done). She described the experience as surprisingly exhilarating, not scary, and said that the plane provided a good supply of blankets for the flight. At the end of her account of the dream, she said to me, "Be sure and tell Norman about this."

I wondered if the dream wasn't a premonition of her ultimate flight of death—at first a chilling ride, then one warmed by the blankets. All I could make of it was that, to her, it was a kind of religious experience, which she wanted to share with Norm— maybe because he was a "man of the cloth" in her mind, even if not in his. I took it as a sign of her acceptance of him and our marriage. She died just a few days later.

After the funeral service, Dad and I wept as we followed Mother's casket up the aisle of the Methodist church and outside.

At the time, Norm—whose work in Charlotte was coming to an end, creating no small amount of anxiety for us—was on an intensive job search up North. He had visited Mother a few times before he left, but he didn't come home for her funeral. He was in New York City after a visit to Pendle Hill, a Quaker study and conference center near Philadelphia. He wrote in his diary: "UN session . . . also visited Harlem . . . Mrs. C. died." I understood that Norman was on a mission on behalf of our family, but that didn't minimize my hurt and disappointment that he wasn't at the funeral. I didn't express my feelings to him, though; he was depressed enough about the job situation and the implications for our future.

One after another, job opportunities failed to materialize. Quaker foundations turned down grant requests for continuing our work in Charlotte. I suggested we could move to Corry and work the five acres Norman owned and loved, maybe start a nursery business there. "But the world doesn't need another nursery business," he protested, adding dismissively, "Anybody can be a gardener."

Norman seemed to sink into a gloomy, fatalistic state of mind. Still recovering from the shock of losing my mother, I was out of touch with just how low his morale had dropped. Years after his death, I was stunned to read his diary entry for June 30, 1961: "Found out about no-go at Barber-Scotia [College] and now I really wonder what I am living for, and what I could ever contribute." The next day, pondering his mother-in-law's death, he added, "I hoped I wouldn't be alive to see this date. I have been thinking about this since before Frances died, wondering if I might be first."

It was a prickly summer, with misunderstandings erupting between some members of the meeting and us. Norm recorded in his diary, "In spite of ourselves we tried the ministry and hate it." He was offered a part-time position teaching Bible at a local high school, for a salary of $3,450, and wrote more hopefully, "A new life begins as a teacher."

Then came another development that captured his energies. Freedom Riders, in a quest to desegregate public transportation in the South, arrived and were hosted by the Charlotte Meeting. But not everyone supported their coming, and Norman commented later that it "almost split" the meeting.

August 27, 1962, was Norman's last day as a "paid Quaker," as he put it. We had to move out of the meetinghouse, and we barely weathered the school year in a duplex on Norm's small salary. By spring, he was job hunting again. Although our marriage was strained by all this, we hung on, bonded by commitment, dogged faith, and Norman's belief in "guided drift."

Finally, as Quakers say, "way opened." While we were co-directing a Quaker summer camp in South China, Maine, with our two small children underfoot, we received word that Norman had been hired as the executive secretary of the Stony Run Friends Meeting in Baltimore. Stony Run was a venerable meeting, established in 1782, with a large membership, which sponsored a retirement home and a Friends school. It offered an exciting new opportunity for Norman.

We moved to Baltimore in the summer of 1962. I gradually conquered my homesickness for North Carolina, and soon our entire family was caught up in the active life of the school and the meeting. Stony Run provided support and valuable experience for Norman's professional growth, but overall he and the meeting were just not the right fit.

As the civil rights movement and growing U.S. military involvement in Vietnam escalated tensions in the nation, Norman brought a radical Quaker posture to a meeting that didn't fully embrace him or his prophetic vision. Officials of its school had decided to integrate classes by just one grade each year, and in 1963 the high school was still segregated. That was unacceptable to Norman and some others in the meeting. His occasional bluntness and lack of social graces exacerbated tensions and divisions.

In the early spring of 1964, Ben and Tina contracted German measles. We had heard that the virus was around, and then suddenly it was on our doorstep. Shortly after the children became ill, I began to experience similar symptoms. Surely, I thought, I couldn't have the disease. Feeling troubled, I went to see our old family doctor, who examined me and said, "I'll give you a shot of gamma globulin, just in case." With that, the symptoms subsided, and I began to feel better.

Soon afterward, my OB/GYN declared that I was pregnant. "I can't be," I protested, and pleaded with her to repeat the test. With a patient smile, the good doctor did just that. After the second test, she reported that, sure enough, I was pregnant indeed.

I wasn't unhappy about having another child; I was just concerned about the timing. Norman's professional future was still insecure, and I would have preferred to wait a year. But that concern faded quickly into the background when I told the doctor about my potential brush with German measles and the gamma globulin shot. She was worried and chagrined that I had been given the injection, because such shots can mask symptoms. She wanted to know if I was aware that German measles might well affect the health and development of my baby, and that its effects are particularly severe in the early weeks of pregnancy.

My head reeled. I knew I may well have contracted German measles during the sixth week of my pregnancy. I was stunned. The doctor said Norman and I should talk it over, sharing our feelings about the potentiality of having a disabled child. Abortions were not routine in those days, but the doctor was on the board of Johns Hopkins Hospital and thought she could effectively argue for an abortion in our case. It would have to be performed no later than the thirteenth week of the pregnancy. We had five weeks to decide.

During the days that followed, Norman and I put our heads and hearts together over this huge decision. From the beginning, Norm was convinced that the baby would be fine. For him, it was a matter of intuition or faith—or both. I worked more with reason and probability. I had to find out what our chances were. We made numerous telephone calls to family members, friends, and doctors. The odds didn't look very good, but I had always considered myself an optimist regarding odds.

Norman's faith that the baby would be all right was encouraging to me. But even more important was our resolve that, if circumstances required it, we could accept the responsibility of a disabled child. Bill, my brother with Down syndrome, has been part of my family since I was fourteen, and I had some responsibility for his care in his early years, before I went off to college. I understood what it means to have a child with special needs in the family. I knew the depth of my family's love for Bill, and his for us. He has given us all many lessons in compassion, patience, and joy, showing us how to take things as they come and live in the moment, and my life has been blessed by his presence in it.

After a lot of prayer, meditation, and information gathering, for me the decision finally came down to one question: Could we request an abortion? When I confronted this question at the deepest level, I knew the answer. I could not see myself walking up the steps of Johns Hopkins for the procedure. We told our doctor that we were going ahead with the pregnancy.

Once the decision was made, I began to relax. Our dear friends and mentors in the meeting, Harry and Mary Cushing Niles, strongly believed in the power of prayer and positive visualization. Harry bought me a little statue of a healthy, fat, seventeenth-century cherub from an art gallery, as well as a small photographic reproduction of Luca della Robbia's fourteenth-century *Madonna and Child*. I put these on a table and prayed by them often.

All the pregnancy signs were good. In a few weeks, it seemed, I began to experience strong movement in my womb—a sign of the baby's vigor and health. On November 11, 1964, just before dawn, I began to have labor pains. Norm and I rushed to Johns Hopkins.

It was an easy birth. Unlike the other two, I was awake during this one. I wanted to know immediately if this baby was healthy, and to be able to help decide what to do if we encountered complications. Emily Fuller arrived big and strong and perfect. When the nurses brought her to me and laid her on my chest, I laughed and wept simultaneously.

Norman and I felt profoundly blessed to have three beautiful children. But like all marriages and families, ours had difficulties and challenges along with the joys. Norman and I should have shared our hearts and our souls more. We should have been more honest with each other. But we were young, and neither of us knew how to be open with our feelings. We knew much more about how to protect each other and ourselves from our strong emotions. Still, our marriage was, overall, loving and full of purpose.

I will be forever grateful that the last one of our eight years together was the best of all that we shared. Emily's arrival in our family brought Norman and me closer, to a place of quiet peace and joy. Because of the perilous circumstances and risks surrounding her birth, I think Emily was an answer to prayer for us, and especially a confirmation of Norman's faith.

Our family was complete a few months later when Norman arrived home late one Saturday, at the end of a long day of community work with Stony Run teenagers in Baltimore's inner city, carrying a puppy. The energetic black-and-brown ball of fluff with white feet was cute, but Norman's timing was terrible. We had responsibility for the care of three young children, one still an infant, and were just a couple of weeks away from making a move to a new home around the corner.

Norman had come upon a mama dog and her litter of Border collie-shepherd puppies and had selected "the prettiest pup" as a gift for the children. Ben and Tina fell instantly in love with her, of course. Norman convinced me to let her spend the night. We arranged a cozy space on the top landing of the basement stairs, with a blanket, an old shoe, and a ticking clock—surely enough comfort for a young puppy. But she yelped and cried most of the night, and by morning I was clear that taking in and training a puppy at this time in our lives was just too much.

I shared my resolve at breakfast. As if sensing what was going on, the pup moved over under the table and laid her little nose on my bare toes. I melted, and then declared that, since it was a Sunday—already a busy day in our family life—she could stay one more night before Norman had to take her back. Whitefoot stayed for seventeen long, precious years. She ran with the graceful ease of a gazelle, slept often stretched out beside one of the children, and looked after Ben, Tina, and Emily as if they were her entrusted flock of sheep.

During Emily's first year, our pediatrician told us that, in terms of development, she was "off the charts." At ten months, she took her first continuous steps. In our big upstairs bedroom, she walked to me, then turned around and walked to Norman, then repeated it, back and forth, several times. All three of us laughed. That moment, just a month before Norman's death, is one of my happiest memories.

Emily's safe arrival and blossoming growth, like Ben's and Tina's, left me in awe. As a young mother, I often heard in my heart echoes of the words of the psalmist, who declared that we are all "wondrously formed." And each of us is a mystery—to others, maybe even to ourselves.

I believe there will always be mystery surrounding Norman's sacrifice, and around Norman himself. If nothing else, he was a paradox. He was dedicated to a life of self-giving, yet was fascinated with the stock market. He resisted "making money" because he felt he might become obsessed with it. He was socially ill at ease, at times off-putting and perplexing in his manner, yet compassionate and concerned about people. He was often frugal to the point of being a pinch-penny, yet was generous with his few possessions. He had a natural dancing rhythm, but couldn't carry a tune. He was intense and serious about life, but had a quirky, off-handed sense of humor. Self-disciplined and even austere, Norman, upon occasion, loved to wear a beret at a rakish angle and enjoy a glass of beer or a cigar.

Norman was a very private person, a loner. When I came across reflections by Carl Jung on his own childhood, I thought of Norman. Jung wrote, "As a child I felt myself to be alone, and I am still, because I know things and must hint at things which others apparently know nothing of, and for the most part do not want to know." Loneliness, wrote Jung, does not come from an absence of people, but from an inability to communicate what one finds most important, or from holding views that others deem inadmissible.

"It is important to have a secret, a premonition of things un-known," Jung continued. "We must sense that we live in a world which in some respects is mysterious; that things happen and can be experienced which remain inexplicable; that not everything which happens can be anticipated." The world, in Jung's view, "has from the beginning been infinite and ungraspable."

Most of us find comfort in the expected; Norman loved the unexpected. As for Jung, for Norman the world was essentially spiritual and numinous, surpassing rational comprehension. Norman's deepest thoughts remained an enigma. In the end, he did something totally astonishing and ungraspable. I believe that, paradoxically, the act that ended his short and intense life some-how made it more whole. But it broke my heart—and Ben's and Tina's—and tore the life of our young family apart.

Norman's graduation photo.

Norman, Anne, Ben, and Christina.

Ben and Norman on the last day of Friends China Camp, Maine, the summer of 1962.

Anne and baby Emily, 1964.

The suffering of the Vietnamese was always on Norman's mind: "What can we do that we haven't done?"

Anne, Ben, and Norman's brother Ralph arrive at Stony Run Friends Meeting in Baltimore for Norman's memorial service, November 6, 1965.

The Pentagon, where Norman died.

Secretary of Defense Robert McNamara later described Norman's death as "one of the darkest moments" of his life.

We received messages from Prime Minister Pham Van Dong and President Ho Chi Minh from North Vietnam. According to the Prime Minister, "Norman Morrison has gone into Vietnamese mythology."

Delegation in the 1970s visiting the Ho Chi Minh Museum, which features a memorial to Norman.

3

"Now His Love Has Spread All Over the World"

The world doesn't need many martyrs. But it needs a few.
—NORMAN MORRISON

When I arrived home with Emily from Ft. Myer, my dear friends Peggy Brick and Nancy Clark were there. Ben and Tina were asleep in Ben's room on the third floor. Neither had wanted to go to bed alone that night. I placed Emily, sleeping soundly, into her crib.

Peggy insisted upon drawing a hot bath for me, then gave me a soothing back rub. Even so, I couldn't sleep. Though Peggy encouraged me to "just let go," I couldn't cry. I was awake most of the night thinking about Norman. I couldn't bear to imagine the pain he must have suffered, if only for a few minutes, or moments.

One thought that visited me over and over was that Norman's spirit was finally free and at peace. That was my prayer for him, more than anything else. An image of Martin Luther King Jr. crept into my mind: the great orator standing in front of the Lincoln Memorial during the August 1963 March on Washington, declaring, "Free at last! Free at last! Thank God Almighty, I'm free at last!" Those words were triumphant; I wanted to believe that Norman's death was a victory. Norman had struggled with his life, and he had wanted so much to make a difference in the world. And now, I believed, he was at home and at peace.

The next morning, I woke up feeling like stone. The children and their needs were the only thing that got me out of bed that day, and for many days to follow. Ben and Tina were still in bed upstairs together. Walking up the narrow stairs to the third floor, I didn't know what I was going to say to my two little ones. I prayed for God's help.

I sat on Ben's bed and gathered them both in my arms. I told them that their Daddy had died to stop a war that was hurting and killing little children like them in a far-off land. I didn't know if I could make them understand, but it was the truth, and I didn't know what else to say.

"But why, Mommy?" asked Tina.

"He did it because he loved them, too."

They were both, poor little ones, in shock. I can't imagine what they thought. Like the rest of us, they didn't know what to do or say. Ben, our practical and quiet child, said nothing.

Tina was trying very hard to make sense of it. In the preceding weeks, she had begun asking questions: "Where do clouds come from?" "What's the sun?" "Where is heaven?" "What happens when you die?" After a long silence, a knowing look spread over her little face, and she exclaimed, "Oh, I understand. Daddy has died, and now his love has spread all over the world."

I held them close, telling them that their Daddy would want them to be brave—a declaration I now regret. My words were a noble effort, but they did not address my children's shocked and broken hearts, or mine. I held back my own tears in an effort to be as brave as I was encouraging them to be.

I know now that we should have cried our hearts out together. Because we did not, our family remained in a state of frozen grief for years. A decade would pass before I would begin to find my tears and get in touch with my deepest feelings. Years more would go by before I would fully understand how deeply wounded Ben and Tina were that their father didn't tell them goodbye.

Perhaps Norman didn't consider saying goodbye to his children. But a more plausible explanation to me is that he would have found that task too emotionally overwhelming, facing an impending loss so great that the thought of it might have deterred him from doing what he believed he needed to do. The children couldn't have physically stopped him if they'd known, but I think just seeing their pain or their panic would have dissuaded him. If Norman had told me what he was planning, I would have done anything to stop him. I would have blocked the door, or called the police, or something . . . anything. I don't know how, but I would have stopped him.

After I explained to the children what had happened, leaving out the most painful of the details, we went downstairs to breakfast. Our house had become filled with concerned friends. Soon Ben disappeared from the table. Several of us went looking for him. I found him, sobbing in the garage, alone and bereft. He had been so close to his dad.

After the terrible task of telling Ben and Tina that they would never see their father again, my only goal for the day was to take Emily to our pediatrician, who confirmed that she was physically unharmed from the ordeal of the day before. I didn't have to decide what else to do. Phone calls, from both friends and strangers, came all day, some with requests for television interviews. One publishing house wanted to do an instant biography of Norman. Camera crews with spotlights camped in front of our home that night, until some kind friend told them to leave.

During those days after Norman's death, I said no to almost every invitation from the media. I was just trying to stay sane, and to protect and mother my children. In retrospect, I realize that we should have left the frenzy of attention and gone away somewhere for a time, just the four of us, to grieve.

The day after Norman's death, a letter arrived in the mail. It was postmarked Washington, D.C., and addressed to me. In Norman's handwriting. I opened it with trembling hands, wondering for an instant if the horror of the day before had been just a nightmare, if Norman was still alive. He must have written it just before he left home for the Pentagon. It said, in part:

> *Dearest Anne, Please don't condemn me. . . . For weeks, even months, I have been praying only that I be shown what I must do. This morning with no warning I was shown, as clearly as I was shown that Friday night in August 1955 that you would be my wife. . . . At least I shall not plan to go without my child, as Abraham did. Know that I love thee but must act for the children in the Priest's village. Norman*

Enclosed with his farewell letter was the article that he had read the previous morning. It was circled with a red pencil. Titled "A Priest Tells How Our Bombers Razed His Church and Killed His People," the searing reflection by French reporter Jean Larteguy had appeared in that week's edition of I. F. Stone's newsletter, reprinted from a Paris magazine. Norman and I had talked about the horror of the event it recounted, just hours before he died.

Larteguy had discovered a French priest, Father Currien, in a hospital bed in a clinic in Saigon. In his hand the priest held a small pyx, a round, metal vessel in which the Blessed Sacrament is carried; it had been pierced by two bullets. Showing it to the reporter, the priest said: "This was the consecrated host. In this war they even shoot God himself."

The people of Duc Co, one of the villages Father Currien served, had been caught in a skirmish between South Vietnamese troops and the Viet Cong guerrilla militia. When the Viet Cong soldiers left, even worse devastation visited the village. "The first bomb fell at 6:05 on my church," the priest recounted. "There was nothing left of it. I ran for shelter to the presbytery, a wooden house adjoining the church. A second bomb crushed it, and I was pinned under the beams. Children cried, women shrieked, and the wounded moaned. They were near me but I could not budge."

Eventually, some of Father Currien's parishioners found him and pulled him out of the wreckage. Together they spent a night under the flooring of the house, while U.S. planes hammered the village with rockets and bombs. Before fleeing, Father Currien buried as best he could seven of his parishioners whom he described as "completely torn to bits." He said gravely: "I had to abandon some wounded and dying. I gave them absolution. I tried to keep alive those who were still alive."

He walked to the village of Pleiku with forty-two women and children, refusing a ride from a Vietnamese colonel who offered to carry the wounded priest to safety and choosing instead to accompany his parishioners on their "way of the cross." Some of the children became so exhausted that they lay down at the side of the road, unable to move. "As for the poor mountain people whose villages and rice granaries have been destroyed," said the priest, "they can live only as wild boars in the forest. I have seen my faithful burned up in napalm. I have seen the bodies of women and children blown to bits. I have seen all my villages razed. By God, it's not possible!" With these words, the priest burst into tears. He railed at the Americans in English, as if they were there to hear him. Then, calmly, he said, "They must settle their accounts with God."

The vision of napalmed bodies and wailing children in Vietnam must have accompanied Norman to the Pentagon. Like the wounded French priest, he believed that we are all accountable to God—for our actions and our inactions. "What can we do that we haven't done?" was Norman's sober, haunting question to me on the day he died. A question for which I had no answer.

What has haunted me in the years since was his decision to take Emily with him. His final letter made reference to the great biblical character Abraham, who, according to the Book of Genesis, was commanded by God to sacrifice his son Isaac as a burnt offering. Deeply conflicted and agonized, Abraham nonetheless obeyed. He built an altar, laid the wood, bound Isaac and placed him on it, then raised his knife to kill his beloved son before torching the wood. But an angel intervened, commanding

Abraham to stop and directing him to a ram caught in a thicket—the replacement sacrifice.

Norman had once called Abraham's action an "unreasonable, unconventional act of faith." It is also widely considered an act of ultimate holy obedience. But in the end, love reigned over obedience—as I believe it did in some mysterious way in the encroaching twilight at the Pentagon on November 2, 1965. I do not know what angel intervened as Norman cradled Emily and prepared to douse himself with kerosene and light a match—but I believe that ultimately it was Norman's love that saved her.

Before leaving our home that day, Norman had stuffed Emily's diaper bag with extra milk, diapers, and pacifiers; he must have known she would need them. Although it remains a mystery why he took her with him, I believe it was important for him to hold onto a child he loved so dearly, and to the family and life she represented, right up to the last moment. Underneath his outward courage, deep inside, I believe Norman had both a fear and a love of life, a willingness to do what he felt compelled to do (in purity of heart, to "will one thing") and a reluctance to leave.

A friend told me years later that she believed Norman "clung to Emily as he was clinging to life." She represented hope to him. She was the only one in the family too young to understand that something was amiss and to object. "In a way," said my friend, "his taking Emily was a testament to his humanity, to his longing and need. Because he was this human, his death was even more courageous to me."

I also believe that Norman felt that Emily was symbolic of the many precious Vietnamese children who were vulnerable victims of the war, who were being destroyed by fires of our nation's making. Though I intuitively understood that, Emily's proximity to danger was horrifying to me. Had she been injured or killed, the tragedy would have been unspeakable, and I may well have found it impossible to forgive Norman.

Norman's letter asked me to try to explain his action to Ben and Tina. Hearing from him after his death sent a shock wave through me. But I also felt profound relief receiving the letter and reading the words he must have written only hours before his death. I was holding in my hands his last statement. It was all Norman. I knew him again in the piercing clarity, confusion, and desperation of his last words—and in his poignant plea that I not condemn him.

Of course our family was devastated by the loss, our lives forever altered. With Norman's death, it was as if a heavy curtain fell upon us, creating a "before" and "after" in our lives. On the surface, the children seemed to be coping well. In those first days, Ben, Tina, and I talked about their father's death—but not nearly enough, or honestly enough. I believed I had no right to grieve or be depressed, and it seemed inappropriate to be angry. Anger had never been easy for me, and it was very difficult to be angry at someone who had just given his life for a cause, especially to try to stop a war.

I felt emotionally frozen over the loss of Norman and distracted by demands from all directions. As the one now responsible for my children, I felt as though everything depended on me. I wondered where I would find the strength to get out of bed every morning and face each day. But I knew that, even though November 2 had changed everything, I had to go on.

Emily's first birthday was fast approaching, just nine days after Norman's sacrifice. On November 11, no matter what else was going on, we were going to celebrate her with a cake-and-ice-cream party at a neighbor's home, just as we had planned. Although I tried to "normalize" our life as much as possible during the days, months, and years that followed, there was always the sense of loss, always the unanswered questions. There was always the deep "Why?"

In countless ways, I could not have gotten through those days and weeks without my friends. They brought over so many casseroles that we had to farm them out to several home freezers. Catherine Taylor, a beloved family friend who was like a grandmother to the children, came every afternoon for several weeks, ate supper with us, and spent the night, leaving each morning after breakfast. She was a joyous person, deeply loved by Ben,

Tina, and Emily, and her presence filled the void a bit and made our evenings special.

Immensely supported by people near and far, by angels and the Holy Spirit, I moved through each day. I had to, for the sake of the children. And I did it for Norman, for the sake of our opposition to the war, to support his sacrifice and carry on his work. Often I could feel Norman's spirit just out ahead, urging me to keep up the struggle for peace.

On November 3, the day after Norman died, a group from the Stony Run Meeting—Allan Brick, Eleanor Webb, Sam Legg, John Roemer, and Hooper Bond—held a press conference at the meetinghouse. They issued a simple and strong statement:

> *As friends of Norman Morrison, we have come to appreciate the depths of his commitment to the way of peace. We have recognized the sincerity of his objections to our country's policies in Vietnam. . . . Norman saw these policies as evil. He found it necessary to protest them, but must have been discouraged that the protests seemed to fall on deaf ears. We believe that Norman's action yesterday must have been motivated by a desperate search to find the way to be heard by the American people and by their leaders. We pray that all people will be able to see beyond the act to the essential message.*

In April 1965, six months before Norman's sacrifice, twenty-five thousand students—matching the number of U.S. troops in Vietnam—had marched on Washington in an effort to stop the war. Despite growing public opposition to the conflict, by the end of the year, 184,000 troops had been deployed to the other side of the world. Many were coming home in body bags. The military draft was raiding a mounting number of American families. News was reaching the United States of our obliteration-bombing campaigns and escalating Vietnamese civilian deaths; of the mining of Haiphong harbor and the massive defoliation of Vietnam's countryside with Agent Orange; of napalm and the "scorched earth" policy of burning villages, destroying livestock and rice stores, and rounding up survivors into "new life hamlets."

Norman ardently preached against the war, planned peace vigils and conferences, lobbied in the halls of Congress, and withheld taxes that supported the conflict. He wrote regularly to politicians, including a few direct pleas to President Lyndon Johnson and his press secretary, Bill Moyers, who had been a seminarian at New College in Edinburgh, Scotland, the year before Norman was there.

On May 6, 1965, Norman wrote to the editor of the *Baltimore Sun*:

> *It is my opinion that any nation which insists that there is no choice but to fight is no longer a great power. . . . All of us are appalled by the human tragedy and suffering involved in Vietnam. . . . The United States has over-extended itself and can only make more enemies by continuing with its present policy of intervening on the side of unpopular and unstable governments in foreign countries.*

Norman was becoming increasingly agonized by the killing of Vietnamese civilians. That our country was knowingly destroying people, villages, and an ancient culture in Vietnam was appalling to us both. Norman could not accept the unspeakable human toll the war was taking on the Vietnamese and on our soldiers. He was convinced that if the war continued, it would take a heavy toll on the soul of America as well. Also, he was afraid that China or the Soviet Union eventually would enter the war on the side of North Vietnam, escalating the conflict into a nuclear World War III. We now know that his fears were not groundless; nuclear options had been officially proposed at our highest military levels.

For those perplexed by his ultimate sacrifice, Norman's own words may be a window into his mind and heart. Fortunately, he left behind plenty of words—lecture notes, articles, letters to the editor, diaries, sermons, and brief messages he had given to Charlotte and Stony Run Friends. After his death, I was surprised to find among his papers an undated document he had titled "Morrison Constitution," which said in part:

> *If we would know God we need also to know our neighbor. To know our neighbor we need to sacrifice something on his behalf. It is the father and Creator of us all that can help us to sufficiently rise above the fears and apprehensions resulting from self-centered living so that we might make necessary sacrifices. In this way we would become a creative means in bringing life and comfort to mankind.*

Norm understood the concept of neighbor broadly. Though he was a consummate individualist—sometimes exasperatingly so—he embraced an understanding of global identity. Because in his eyes all people were part of one human family, to him the sufferings of the people of Vietnam were sufferings of members of his own family. His loyalty to the world community encompassed his loyalty to our family.

For Norman, the individual was ultimately accountable to God, and then to one's family and faith community. Loyalty to the nation, state, or any other institution was of lesser importance—and resistance was necessary when those institutions contradicted conscience. David H. Fischer, writing in *Albion's Seed* about the history of Quakers, could have been describing Norman in this observation: "Quakers insisted that a believing Christian had a sacred duty to stand against evil in government, and that individual conscience was the arbiter of God's truth."

Of utmost importance to Norman was obedience to one's internal authority, as informed by God through the Inward Light or Inward Christ. He believed that a divine hand was guiding lives. On the day he died, while preparing notes to teach a class, he wrote, "The church of the spirit is always being built. It possesses no other kind of power and authority than the power and authority of personal lives, formed into a community by the vitality of the divine-human encounter."

With all his heart, Norman wanted to be used as one of God's redemptive agents in society. To Norman, holy obedience meant being willing to take risks, sowing seeds in faith without knowing what fruits might come. He understood the well-nigh impossible challenge of unconditional love as Christ's way of sacrificial obedience. He preached in a sermon in Charlotte, "Doing God's will by bringing love and truth into the world for mankind will always end in crucifixion when it is done as thoroughly and completely as Christ did it."

However, for Norman, death was not the end of individual existence. In remarks at a memorial service for a prominent member of Stony Run Meeting, whose suicide in early 1965 shook Norman and the meeting, Norman said of his friend: "His many skills are treasures which we believe in God's enormous universe will be preserved. In life and in death he exercised the freedom of choice which is the very essence of living in this world." Death, in Norman's understanding, was not something to be feared, because Christ overcame the power of death through his resurrection and thus revealed the triumph of love over evil.

While Norman valued integrity, simplicity, and humility, he placed little value on respectability. He wrote in the October 1963 Stony Run newsletter:

> *Those who have lived out their lives in unrespectability because they followed the promptings of the Inner Light have provided the fruits of Quakerism today. Our greatest service for the future will be measured by our ability to tolerate, accept, or support, with as much love and understanding as possible, individuals within our Society who make faithful response to new light.*

Norman's words illuminate his commitments, but surely his clearest statement was expressed in his last act, a combination of both profound hope and wrenching desperation. Ultimately, Norman's was a soul burdened beyond endurance with the world's suffering. Almost a decade after he died, I heard from a

Friend who had been with him at the Philadelphia Quaker center, Pendle Hill, only a few days before he gave up his life. She
still had vivid memories of Norman speaking at a worship meeting there:

> *Never before have I been in the presence of such inner suf-
> fering. . . . He pleaded with us to enter his pain, acknowl-
> edge its depth and reality. He implored us to DO some-
> thing, as if the handful of people gathered there had the
> power to stem the war. Perhaps what he was really asking
> us for was some sense of hope, something he could cling to
> so as not to be engulfed in his own feeling of pain and
> powerlessness. The immensity of his feeling seemed to stag-
> ger and stun us. Who could break the silence to offer [a
> response] sufficient to the need that had been expressed? I
> think we all felt immobilized in the presence of such depth
> of desperation. Even our pooled resources could not have
> filled the void he gave words to, the ache in his spirit. . . .
> We tried to comfort, but comfort was a puny offering and
> we had no insight profound enough. . . . We were unable
> to build a bridge of communication to his feeling. He
> seemed lost to us at the very moment when he seemed to
> need another human's help the most.*

On November 4, 1965, a small group of Norman's friends from
Baltimore held a memorial service for him outside the Pentagon,
at the place and time of his death two days earlier. The two-hour
prayer service included readings from Gandhi, Albert Camus,
Martin Buber, and Henry David Thoreau. The friends made a
public statement, saying, "We do not necessarily approve of persons burning themselves to death. . . . But we are sympathetic to
all expressions of concern about the suffering of humanity." They
added that they felt that Norman was "a great man . . . who believed that his self-sacrifice was a giving, not a taking of life."

A memorial service for Norman was held on November 6 at
the Stony Run Meetinghouse. Anticipating a large crowd, the

overseers arranged for the use of two extra rooms in addition to the main meeting room. All three were needed. Norman's mother, Hazel, was there, as well as his brother Ralph, who came from Ethiopia, where he and his wife, Sue, were serving in the Peace Corps. My Dad and brother Bill didn't come until a few days later. I was in a daze, and the memorial service was mostly a blur to me.

Harry Niles came home immediately from India for the memorial service. He offered these remarks:

> *Norman acted in accord with the best Quaker traditions.*
> *. . . It is the Quaker tradition to follow the Inner Light and to do what one truly believes is right for him to do, even in the face of public misunderstanding. . . . Norman Morrison challenged our government, not with physical force but with emotional and spiritual force. He challenges each of us, especially those of us who are Quakers, not necessarily to do with our bodies what he did, but to do with our lives what he did with his—namely, to give them for the highest service to God and our fellowman as each looks for and finds for himself what that service should be.*

Controversy raged in the media about whether Norman was a fanatic or a saint, his death a suicide or an act of heroism. A few commentators declared it an act of insanity. One reflected, "Beneath his deep convictions lay a form of paranoia." A psychiatrist wrote in the *Baltimore Sun* that Norman was likely offering himself as a sacrifice to expiate the sin of our society and to impress upon our nation its sinfulness.

Life magazine's Loudon Wainwright wrote a critical essay, calling Norman's sacrifice "a deranged act" and "a truly pitiful death." Wainwright did, however, concede that "Mr. Morrison's death—however vain, insane, or otherwise deplorable most people will find it—will doubtless lead to even more consideration" of the "condition of the American conscience in regard to Vietnam."

A letter addressed to Defense Secretary Robert McNamara and the Joint Chiefs of Staff from physician Marian E. Manly arrived at the Pentagon a few days after Norman's death:

> *Gentlemen: It is easy to dismiss Norman Morrison's dreadful act as the meaningless self-destruction of a deranged fanatic. It was desperate; it was futile; but it was not meaningless. What he was trying to say was: "See what it is like for a man to die by fire. See it for yourselves. You, who make impersonal war, devising strategies and tactics in your air-conditioned offices, look and see!"*

A Washington radio editorial broadcast on November 4 and 5 called Norman's act "unfair and unjust to an extreme degree because he—and the people who think like him—do not really appreciate the hard, inescapable realities of a national policy. . . . What Mr. Morrison did may have been brave. It was also grossly cruel to the decision-makers in this capital." The November 6 Religion section of the *Baltimore Sun* featured a forum by several local members of the clergy. Two condemned Norman's action, one refused to pass judgment, and the fourth said he felt that its impact would be negligible, because "modern man has become hardened to violent death. . . . I am afraid that such self-sacrifice is usually wasted."

But negative conclusions seemed to be the exception. I was astonished that the media and the public were as sympathetic as they were. I had imagined that the majority would have concluded that Norman was insane, but that seemed to be the minority report. The Presbyterian Ministers' Fund, with which Norman had a five-thousand-dollar life insurance policy, promptly and voluntarily sent me a check for the full amount, though the policy contained the usual exclusionary clause for suicide.

Days passed after Norman's death, and I still hadn't wept over my profound loss. Maybe I felt that with a war going on and people dying every day in Vietnam, my tears would be

self-indulgent and a sign of weakness. Instead, I threw myself into work to end the war. I shared Norman's resolve, reflected in these words I wrote in the November 11 edition of the Stony Run newsletter: "Norman Morrison was convinced that the control and ultimate elimination of war is an imperative of this century. He considered war itself—and the hatred and passions it inspires—as the real enemy of the peoples of Vietnam and the United States. He gave his life as witness to this belief."

One of the most painful things for me in the weeks and months after Norman's death was having to go over it again and again with Ben and Tina. With time, they found more questions to ask: "Wasn't there a better way?" "Why did Daddy have to be the one?" And one day Tina uttered the heartbreaking truth: "It didn't stop the war."

My family and Norman's did their best to be supportive, but they too were devastated. Most of my relatives were quiet in the wake of Norman's sacrifice. I think they were deeply embarrassed and sad for the children and me. One exception was my cousin Emily Neary, who wrote me a beautiful letter:

> *Right now I am almost crying because I have realized, after two days of thinking about Norman and talking about him with my friends and family, that so few people care deeply enough about anything to understand how he could do so noble an act. . . . What he did in the cause of peace and love is so noble as to rank him with a few great people in the history of the world. I am very proud of your brave husband and have told everyone I know so, and I am proud of you for being so strong and for continuing Norman's work. . . . We feel the war in Vietnam must stop for the same reasons you do. We want love and understanding in the world, not killing and hate.*

Letters with similar sentiments flooded in from all corners. With the enormous assistance of Eleanor Webb and other friends, I was able to respond to many of them. Quakers were

especially responsive. The news of Norman's death was particularly shocking in places where we had connections, but questions raised by his action reverberated within Friends meetings around the country and beyond.

Though we Quakers have a valiant history of suffering for our beliefs, some Friends said that because Norman's action involved violence to himself, it was not in accord with pacifism or peaceful witness. A stumbling block for others was Emily's presence and the potential of violence done to an innocent child. Still another difficulty for some was the fact that Norman had acted alone, without the approval or release of his meeting. That Stony Run Meeting would not have approved—indeed, would have taken action to prevent Norman's sacrifice—is, to me, beyond question.

Yet the letters I received were overwhelmingly sympathetic and supportive. Some contained money to support our family or for the memorial fund that we established at Friends World College in Norman's memory to further his vision of peace. A couple in Los Gatos, California, wrote:

> *Your husband was a casualty of an undeclared war for which our President bears the responsibility but for which we all bear the shame. Unfortunately, there will be no veteran's pension or other government benefits for you and your children. Will you then please accept our check in aid of your children's education? As parents our hearts go out to them and to you.*

A member of the Cambridge, Massachusetts, Meeting wrote to tell me how "fiercely proud" she was of Norman's sacrifice, which she described as "an act of courage that will go down in Quaker annals throughout the years." She wrote, "We grieve with you, but we also rejoice that a Friend should make so heroic a sacrifice as witness to his beliefs."

The national Friends Coordinating Committee on Peace held a memorial service in Washington on November 21. One speaker

quoted a letter he had received from a young Friend who had written, "Must we sit quietly by wringing our hands and resign ourselves to complicity in the barbaric terror and torture now being perpetrated in our name?" Norman, said the speaker, "found a thing *to do.*" Another speaker reflected:

> *In a society where it is normal for human beings to drop bombs on human targets, where it is normal to spend fifty percent of the individual's tax dollar on war, . . . where it is normal to give war toys for Christmas, where it is normal to have twelve times overkill capacity, Norman Morrison was not normal. He said, "Let it stop. . . . Let us be abnormal in the sense that Jesus and Gandhi were abnormal. Let us practice the law of love."*

I heard from the Edinburgh Meeting in Scotland and a Hindu in Bangalore, India; from friends in Charlotte and Pittsburgh; from strangers in Nashville and Atlanta and Berkeley, California. Letters arrived from Egg Harbor, New Jersey, and Tenants Harbor, Maine. A letter was delivered from Holzhausen, Germany, its envelope addressed simply to "Frau Morrison, Washington, USA." People sent poems and prayers, assuring me of their wishes for my strength and for the well-being of the children.

Marguerite Smith, Norm's beloved teacher, wrote, "It strengthens my conviction that the boy whom I once taught Latin here in Chautauqua High School grew to be a very brave man." I received messages from former students of Norman's, from the mother of a young woman he had dated in high school, and from a Baltimore friend who had faced the same German measles scare as I had during my pregnancy with Emily. She wrote, "By his sacrifice of so good a life, Norman has shown the courage, universal love, and vision of the great religious prophets of the past, and his act has eternal meaning. . . . I pray that God's love is sustaining you."

From Susan Smith—a close friend and founder of the Friends Meeting in Durham, where I first encountered Quakerism and

where Norman and I said our marriage vows—came a message that quoted Rufus Jones: "The prophet . . . cannot give people what they want. He is under an inescapable compulsion to give them what his soul believes to be true." Susan's message applauded Norman's "courage to make the supreme sacrifice in order to accomplish his purpose." She wrote, "Although I am terribly saddened by this event, it is good to know that Quakers of this caliber still exist."

A friend of mine from graduate school posed this question: "What of the man so made that he doesn't possess the horrid anesthesia of our civilization, the power to look and not see, to hear and not know?" A close friend of Norman's from Wooster College said that, knowing Norm as he did during the formative period of some of his beliefs, he had no doubt that "his final act was the result of a perfectly rational decision and that his death was an affirmation of those ideals that he held and lived throughout this life." This friend offered his hope that "the focus of our shock" be not on Norman's act but on "the conditions in the world and in American society that made Norman believe that this sacrifice was necessary."

A letter signed by forty people arrived from Pendle Hill. It said in part, "We want you to know that we feel no need to pass judgment on his action. The question now is, what about ours? Our souls have been stirred and searched over and over again these days." In a similar vein, a Baltimore Friend wrote of Norman, "It is up to the rest of us, now, to see that he did not die in vain." The Friend confessed that, since learning of Norman's death, he had been persistently challenging himself with two questions: "And how deeply do *you* feel the suffering and tragedy of the world? What sacrifices would *you* make to stab men's spirits wide awake?"

An article about Norman and other war protesters was published in *The Christian Century* in January 1966. It brought this response from a reader in Detroit: "Norman Morrison had found out over long years of talking that words are cheap and seldom heard. At last he simply converted his life into a word which would carry. I heard him; I'm sure Pres. Johnson and everyone in

our government heard him. . . . Who is prepared to say this act was futile?"

Peace organizations and individuals wrote, saying they were increasing their efforts against the war, writing letters to editors and members of Congress, and holding vigils and teach-ins. A friend from Duke who was teaching at Stephens College in St. Louis initiated a fast for peace there. A fraternity brother of Norman's, a United Church of Christ pastor in Cleveland, wrote that his parish had recommitted itself to peacemaking and sent this personal encouragement: "There are always the scoffers and detractors. May your heart never be swayed by them."

A Japanese woman working for peace wrote that Norman's death "imprinted in our hearts a mark which will never fade and which encourages us to do what we believe to be right. . . . No one can erase your grief, I am sure, but please understand that there are millions of people in the world who share your grief and are determined to make the world a better place for all of us to live in. Mr. Morrison's death will not be lost."

A Quaker conscientious objector wrote to our family from his prison cell in Springfield, Missouri: "The five of you are involved in a sacrifice which cannot be measured. . . . You do not bear the sacrifice in vain. Since 1961 I have tried to devote my life to peace action; if ever I waver (and I do) I'll know anew others are giving far more, and be renewed by the meaning and spirit of the act which now is also your individual grief, and ours. . . . Therefore today is a day I am proud to be a Quaker."

One of the most moving letters came from a friend of Norman's who was in Bien Hoa, South Vietnam, fighting in the war. He had written Norman on October 31, 1965, justifying U.S. involvement there. I didn't receive that letter until after Norman's death. Another soon followed, in which the young man expressed regret about his previous letter and mentioned hearing news of Norman's sacrifice and my public statement over Armed Forces Radio. He wrote:

It is clear that I, in fully (though reluctantly) supporting that against which Norman hurled himself, am equally responsible for his death, in a more fundamental way than by the mere pulling of a trigger. I should expect and welcome your bitterest hatred against me and all those whom I support and with whom I work, for it would give vent to your grief, and blunt the sharpness of the loss. But I know you are of the conviction that only love can overcome death and evil, and will not permit yourself the luxury of hate.

Few men have Norman's immediate and urgent concern for people. His act of sacrifice for this concern testifies indeed that he was a great, as well as a loving, human being. My respect for him is very great, my sympathy for you is deep and sincere, and my concern over the issue here is sharpened and deepened.

A Chautauqua friend applauded Norman's commitment, ending her letter: "As for you, you are left to pick up the pieces. It's no help to be told you are strong at a time like this, but you are. I was so proud of you—your pictures, your public statement. And my heart broke for you, too." Members of the Baltimore branch of the Women's International League for Peace and Freedom said, "We feel overwhelmed by the personal sacrifice this cause has required of you." A dear, elderly friend at Stony Run wrote to me, "If your appearance and your actions really mirror your inmost self, your inner peace and sense of the presence of God must have wonderfully met the test of suffering."

If all that was so, it was only by the grace of God and the angels. And because of a wide network of friends that was supporting and upholding me. I felt that I needed to be true to their trust, to be strong and not to let them down. But it felt strange and uncomfortable that I was no longer living a private life, with a private grief. I struggled with that reality constantly.

Over the years, I learned that Norman's act touched more hearts than I will ever know. I believe that the letters I received after his death spoke for a greater, silent group of people who were moved by his sacrifice and were thinking of and praying for us. I treasured each of those letters. I could never adequately describe the inspiration and strength they gave me. They made the difference between despair and hope.

In early December 1965, I wrote a letter to thank my friends for their outpouring of sympathy and love—for tangible gifts of letters and poetry, unseen gifts of prayer and thought, as well as their many new and diligent efforts in the work of building peace and understanding. "Without them," I wrote, "the burden of loss and grief would have been much heavier. With them you have assured me that Norman's self-giving was not in vain; that it was worth the grief; indeed, that it gives occasion for joy in affirming 'the silent goodness of humanity.'"

I reflected, "This death, as any other, has insisted that the deeper levels of existence be confronted, with honesty, compassion, and commitment to what conscience demands of each of us. There is much evidence both here and abroad that Norman's voice was clearly heard." I ended with these words—still my prayer today: "My hope is that through this experience our hearts have become more sensitive, our wills more responsive, and our lives more authentic."

A passage from T. S. Eliot's *Murder in the Cathedral* seemed perfect to include in my letter:

> *You think me reckless, desperate and mad.*
> *You argue by results, as this world does,*
> *To settle if an act be good or bad.*
> *You defer to the fact. For every life and every act*
> *Consequence of good and evil can be shown.*
> *And as in time results of many deeds are blended*
> *So good and evil in the end become confounded.*
> *It is not in time that my death shall be known;*
> *It is out of time that my decision is taken*
> *If you call that decision*
> *To which my whole being gives entire consent.*
> *I give my life*
> *To the Law of God above the Law of Man.*

Those who do not the same
How should they know what I do? . . .
We are not here to triumph by fighting,
        by stratagem,
    or by resistance,
Not to fight with beasts as men.
We have fought the beast
And have conquered.
We have only to conquer
Now, by suffering.

Later that month, I asked Harry Niles to write to Col. Charles S. Johnson Jr.—one of the men from the Pentagon who had tried to smother the flames engulfing Norman—to thank him for his bravery and to express my concern and hope that his hands had healed. Col. Johnson responded with appreciation and an assurance that he was fine. He wrote, "My only regret is that I was unable to do more."

His letter also said, "You may not be aware that there was another person involved, S/Sgt. Robert C. Bundt. . . . This young airman contributed as much as I, received more serious burns than I and was not identified except as 'an unidentified sergeant' for several days." I wrote to Sgt. Bundt to thank him after reading in the newspaper that he had been awarded a commendation medal for his effort to save Norman. Robert Bundt's neck had puffed up from the intense heat, leaving him with a permanent scar. In an interview years after Norman's death, he still choked with emotion when he recounted seeing Norman in the column of fire.

Five days after Norman's sacrifice at the Pentagon, five pacifists demonstrating with fifteen hundred other antiwar protesters burned their draft cards at Union Square in New York City. A counter-demonstrator rushed toward the five men with a fire extinguisher, dousing them and their burning cards.

Exactly a week after Norman's death, Roger LaPorte, a twenty-two-year-old member of the Catholic Worker movement, went to the United Nations Plaza at dawn. He sat cross-legged in front of the Isaiah Wall, inscribed with words from the prophet: "They shall beat their swords into ploughshares, neither shall they study war anymore." He poured two gallons of kerosene over his head and struck a match. UN guards putting out the flames asked him why he did it. LaPorte replied: "I am against war, all wars. I did this as a religious action." As he was being treated for critical burns in a New York hospital, the city went dark in the great power blackout of 1965. Roger LaPorte died two days later. I was deeply moved and saddened by his sacrifice. He was a very young man.

Norman was not the first American to burn himself in protest of the war. On March 16, 1965, eighty-two-year-old Alice Herz, a Quaker and Unitarian Universalist, had set herself on fire on a Detroit street corner shortly after the first U.S. combat troops landed at Da Nang. She told the firefighter attending her in the ambulance, "I did it to protest the arms race all over the world." She carried a note that denounced "the use of high office by our President in trying to wipe out small nations" and that declared her intention "to call attention to this problem by choosing the illuminating death of a Buddhist." Herz died ten days later. Herz's action got little media attention, perhaps because there were no visible family members or others to interpret her sacrifice. When Norman and I had talked about it, we just shook our heads sadly.

We had been aware that, in June 1963, an elderly Buddhist monk named Thich Quang Duc had self-immolated on a crowded street in Saigon. He was drawing attention to the extremely repressive policies of the U.S.-supported Diem government in South Vietnam, particularly its persecution of Buddhists. Between four hundred and five hundred nuns and monks in saffron robes, a few using loudspeakers to announce their demands to the South Vietnamese government and the world, surrounded Quang Duc as he sat in the lotus position.

Two monks poured petrol over his head and robe. Others fed peppermint oil to the fire to suppress the smell of burning flesh.

Associated Press reporter Malcolm Browne's photograph of the monk in flames was one of the most haunting and searing images of the war. It was reported that the photograph was on President Kennedy's desk the next morning.

Thich Quang Duc's heart, which was not destroyed, was retrieved, enshrined, and treated as a sacred relic. His self-immolation became a catalyst for escalating protests, shifting the political climate in Saigon. Just two months after his death, another monk immolated himself in Phanthiet, about a hundred miles from Saigon.

The self-immolation of Thich Nu Thanh Quang, a Buddhist nun, inspired a demonstration of twenty thousand people in Saigon and a series of eight other self-immolations by monks and nuns throughout the major cities of Vietnam. Stirred to action by their religious leaders, formerly terrified and passive Vietnamese citizens flooded the streets, demanding change. Most political commentators acknowledged that growing opposition to U.S. support of the corrupt Diem government and the fall of the regime in November of 1963 were linked to the Buddhist protests and their popular support among the Vietnamese people.

Sacrifice by self-immolation is terribly difficult for most of us Westerners to comprehend. It is not part of our culture, as it is within the Buddhist tradition of Vietnam, in which it is considered the strongest possible statement of one's conscience through suffering. There is, however, a reference in one of the most familiar chapters of the Bible. In the thirteenth chapter of Paul's First Letter to the Corinthians, he begins with a list of exceptional gifts and acts—speaking in tongues, possessing prophetic powers, understanding mysteries, having faith sufficient to move mountains, giving away all possessions. The list ends with, "And if I hand over my body to be burned, but do not have love, I gain nothing." (Later translations, perhaps finding the phrase troubling or obscure, changed it to, "If I hand over my body so that I may boast . . . ") A friend of mine reflected that Paul should have added another verse: "Those who give their bodies to be

burned with love light a light—a candle, perhaps, in the darkness—that shows the way that we cannot foresee."

Surely the Christian understanding of Jesus' sacrifice on the
cross also has relevance. Jesus said to his disciples and the
crowds: "If any want to become my followers, let them deny
themselves and take up their cross and follow me. For those who
want to save their life will lose it, and those who lose their life
for my sake, and for the sake of the gospel, will save it" (Mark
8:34–35). On the night before his crucifixion, Jesus told his disciples, "No one has greater love than this, to lay down one's life
for one's friends" (John 15:13). Self-sacrifice—a life freely given
for the sake of others—may be the ultimate form of love, in any
tradition.

Rabbi Abraham Heschel, who was in the forefront of opposition to the Vietnam War, denounced the "evil of indifference."
In introducing Martin Luther King Jr. to a convention of Jewish
rabbis, he declared: "Mere knowledge or belief is too feeble to
be a cure for man's hostility to man, man's tendency to fratricide.
The only remedy is *personal sacrifice*, to abandon, to reject what
seems dear, even plausible, like prejudice, for the sake of a greater
truth, to do more than I am ready to understand for the sake of
God."

Harry Niles heard of Norman's self-immolation in India,
while he was on his way to New Delhi to visit a Hindu friend
who had been an associate of Mahatma Gandhi. Harry told the
news to her. "Oh," she said, "that is not a suicide at all, but an
obsessive *satyagraha*." When he asked her to explain, she said
that *satyagraha* is "the following of truth as one sees it completely and without reservation. He was obsessed by the feeling
that he had to witness to what he believed to be right."

The Buddha regarded the world of human experience as essentially one of suffering, with sacrifice at the heart of the universe. Suffering and sacrifice, he taught, are among the ways we
nurture and preserve one another, bear one another's burdens,
tenderly hold each other and our tears. Each time we lovingly
give of ourselves for the sake of another, for the sake of the

world, we sacrifice. The beauty and the wonder are that this brings joy; that suffering and joy are linked together. Indeed, suffering and sorrow may be necessary in order to awaken us to life.

A few months after Norman died, a friend sent me a copy of a letter to Martin Luther King Jr. from Thich Nhat Hanh, the renowned Vietnamese Buddhist monk, teacher, and activist, published in June 1965. In his letter, Nhat Hanh explains the meaning of self-immolation within the Buddhist culture. It was extremely helpful to me in understanding Norman's act:

> *The self-burning of Vietnamese Buddhist Monks in 1963 is somehow difficult for the Western Christian conscience to understand. The press spoke then of suicide, but in essence, it is not. It is not even a protest. What the monks said in the letters they left before burning themselves aimed only at alarming, at moving the heart of the oppressors, and at calling the attention of the world to the suffering endured then by the Vietnamese. To burn oneself by fire is to prove that what one is saying is of the utmost importance.*
>
> *The Vietnamese monk, by burning himself, says with all his strength and determination that he can endure the greatest of sufferings to protect his people. . . . To express will by burning oneself, therefore, is not to commit an act of destruction but to perform an act of construction, that is, to suffer and to die for the sake of one's people. There is nothing more painful than burning oneself. To say something while experiencing this kind of pain is to say it with the utmost of courage, frankness, determination and sincerity. . . .*
>
> *What he really aims at is the expression of his will and determination, not death. . . . The monk who burns himself has lost neither courage nor hope; nor does he desire non-existence. On the contrary, he is very courageous and hopeful and aspires for something good in the future. He does not think that he is destroying himself; he believes in*

> *the good fruition of his act of self-sacrifice for the sake of others. Like the Buddha in one of his former lives . . . who gave himself to a hungry lion which was about to devour her own cubs, the monk believes he is practicing the doctrine of highest compassion by sacrificing himself in order to call the attention of, and to seek help from, the people of the world.*

As was true for those monks, Norman's body became a compassionate flame, a torch that illuminated truth, bringing to light the suffering that many wanted to keep hidden. It signaled with compelling urgency our need to find a way out of the darkness of war.

Writing my annual Christmas letter to friends and family only a few weeks after Norman's death was a challenge. But I wrote it on the wings of the love and support we had received. I needed to respond and, most of all, to say thank you: "This Christmas it is immensely difficult to find words for you because my heart is full and thoughts are soul-size. The shallow layers have been cut away and life is revealed in its deeper dimensions. Grief and joy have been our companions; grief for our incomparable loss and his sacrifice, and joy in beholding man in utter commitment, in holy obedience."

I ended with a passage from Sophocles' *Oedipus at Colonus*:

> *Oedipus: I come to give you something, and the gift*
> *Is my own beaten self: no feast for the eyes;*
> *Yet in me is a more lasting grace than beauty.*
>   —Scene III
> *Chorus: He is gone, poor man?*
> *Messenger: You may be sure he has left this world.*
> *Chorus: By god's mercy, was his death a painless one?*
> *Messenger: That is the thing that seems so marvelous.*

You know, for you were witnesses, how he
Left this place with no friend leading him,
Acting, himself, as guide for all of us. . . .
"I know it was hard my children. And yet one
        word
Frees us of all the weight and pain of life:
That word is love. Never shall you have more
From any man than you have had from me. . . ."
. . . .
Messenger: "Now let the weeping cease;
Let no one mourn again.
These things are in the hands of God."
                                    —Scene VIII, *passim*

4

"Courage"

*When we have conquered the fear
of death, we can face anything that
life may have in store for us.*
—NORMAN MORRISON

*I*n the months after Norman's death, I devoted myself to trying to end the war and to promoting Quaker humanitarian assistance for both North and South Vietnam. I developed a close relationship with the American Friends Service Committee, joining its National Peace Education Committee in the fall of 1966, and later its board of directors. At times, my life seemed almost overwhelmed by letters from abroad, late-night phone calls from people in the forefront of peacemaking, and daily news of the grinding war and the suffering it caused. There was so much to think about, to grieve, and to respond to.

I know, in retrospect, that living at such an intense level of engagement pulled my attention away from Ben, Tina, and Emily, and that is now a source of deep sadness and regret for me. Not only had they paid the severe price of losing their father, they continued to pay a price as a result of my commitment to try to bring an end to the suffering of the children in Vietnam and the children in America whose fathers were coming home wounded or dead.

A source of healing during those difficult days was a rekindled relationship with Bill Beidler, a gifted and generous friend from our days in Charlotte. In 1961, Bill, Norman, and I had jointly purchased a few acres of land in the mountains of western North Carolina. Bill built a cabin there, which became a place of retreat for us all. Bill had an encyclopedic intellect and a contagious enthusiasm. He encouraged my intellectual pursuits and became a kind of soul companion to Norman and me.

Bill and I drew closer after Norman's death. Both the children and I needed the love and security he offered. In June 1967 we were married in a simple Quaker ceremony in Baltimore, at the home of Harry and Mary Cushing Niles. The children had known "Uncle Bill" over the years as part of our family, and they shared a mutual affection. Soon after the wedding, we moved back to Charlotte, where Bill had a job teaching philosophy and world religions at Queens College. Our family was brightened by this union, by the stability it gave us, and by the prospect of starting a new life in familiar territory with Bill's loving support. I was comforted to be back among old friends, and nearer to my dad and brother Bill in Granite Falls.

Our family plunged back into life in Charlotte, dividing our energies among home, school, college, the Friends meeting, and the wider community. Bill and I became increasingly active in local antiwar activities. He and several others in the meeting counseled young men of draft age who, as an act of conscience, chose not to participate in the war. I joined this effort, passing out leaflets about the counseling service at the local military induction center.

The times were moving and turbulent in so many ways. My feminist consciousness was widening, partly through involvement with a new group of women friends, other young mothers who sent their preschool children to Charlotte's progressive and racially diverse Open Door School. Several of us organized a carpool and became close, sharing what was going on in our lives and in the world. The war, the civil rights movement, fair-housing efforts, women's liberation, and social change were all topics of intense discussion and occasional action among my friends and also at the Friends meeting.

In the summer of 1970, Bill accepted a position in the Department of Religion and Philosophy at Guilford College, a Quaker school in Greensboro, North Carolina, precipitating another move. On the surface, we were a happy family. But the children and I continued to suffer inwardly from the loss of Norman. I held inside much unexpressed grief, as well as some anger and guilt. Because I didn't know how to handle my own feelings very well, I couldn't help the children with theirs.

Ben, who was eleven years old, had a difficult time that fall adjusting to a new school. He had always been a bright, earnest, sensitive child. When he was younger and I had to discipline him on occasion, his eyes would immediately well up with tears.

A few months after Tina was born, when Ben was only seventeen months old, I snapped a photograph of him, dressed in his hand-me-down winter overcoat and cap, on the sidewalk in front of our house in Charlotte. He was feeding a rubber doll with a tiny bottle, an expression of intent seriousness on his small face. As soon as he was allowed, Ben pushed Tina around in a stroller with responsibility and proprietorship. Before long, he was carrying her with ease. Over time, Ben developed a wry sense of humor, which he usually expressed through teasing or mild trickery on his younger sisters, often to their consternation.

Ben had been strong and physically robust from birth. As an infant, he grew quickly into wearing husky-sized clothing. When scarcely more than a toddler, he astonished Norman and me by lifting and moving heavy objects, including a wooden crate of empty soda bottles he encountered one day. As he got older, he became a pro at puzzles, solving complicated physical tasks that stymied others. He was a builder of sand and snow castles, of forts and go-carts and kites. Ben was always hammering away at something. Someone once said, admiringly, "Ben thinks with his hands."

He was like his dad in that way. Ben especially loved helping Norman with outdoor projects, such as tending flowers and transplanting trees. His dad passed on to him his love of work and nature, as well as his green thumb—and more important, his courage and determination. When Norman died, Ben lost not only a father but also a close pal. I fear it was a wound that never healed.

Although Ben was physically strong, he was never drawn to competitive sports, and he didn't do well at them. When he started middle school in Greensboro in 1970, his physical education class was a challenge. The P.E. teacher and coach was a former Marine sergeant, with a crew cut and a brusque manner. He declared that he was going to "whip all these little boys into a great team."

Ben's hair was a little long, and so was his best friend's. The coach started calling them girls' names, harassing and embarrassing them. Ben would come home and tell us about it. And from time to time, he said that he didn't feel like going to school, claiming that his leg hurt. Bill and I went and talked to the principal. The coach denied humiliating the boys, but the harassment stopped. We thought that Ben would feel fine then about going to school.

But one morning he announced, "Mom, I can't go to school, my leg hurts too bad." The pain around his knee seemed severe. We took him directly to a bone specialist in Greensboro, whom we knew personally; he was able to see Ben that day. The doctor examined Ben, and without even ordering further tests, declared that this was something serious, suspecting a rare form of bone cancer known as osteogenic sarcoma. He was an older doctor, with many years in medical practice. He told us, "This is very rare. I might have seen twenty-five cases in my whole lifetime of practice."

We were shocked and stricken, asking ourselves over and over, how could it be? Why Ben? He had always been so healthy, so strong. And thus began a new battle, our most difficult one of all—an incredible challenge for Ben and me and our entire family that would last almost five years.

The doctor encouraged us to look beyond Greensboro for treatment. We got on the phone and called around to family and friends. We discovered that the National Institutes of Health (NIH) near Washington, D.C., had a research-and-treatment program for osteogenic sarcoma. Bill and I immediately made plans to take Ben there. Friends came and stayed with Tina and Emily.

Ben was admitted to the NIH program, which, as government-sponsored research, was free of charge to us. That was the up side. The down side was that we had to agree completely to the program's protocol. Even if we heard of a slightly different treatment that sounded better to us, once we entered the program we had to stay with it. We talked with several patients who were already in the program. Most were young; osteogenic sarcoma generally strikes people under the age of thirty. None of them was having very good results. The rate of cure was very low.

The NIH doctors' plan was to remove Ben's leg. We received this news just days after learning that Ben was suffering from this life-threatening illness. We were in a state of shock. We committed ourselves to getting all the information that we possibly could about Ben's disease and putting all our effort toward making the right decisions.

The night before Ben was to have the surgery to amputate his leg, I was in an NIH elevator and overheard a conversation between doctors about Ben's biopsy and the slides of his tissue. The histologist, or tissue specialist, said that he noticed a slight variation in Ben's cells compared to regular osteogenic sarcoma. I asked one of the doctors what that meant. He told me that it indicated that Ben had Ewing's tumor, a particular type of osteogenic sarcoma that is more responsive to chemotherapy and radiation. He mentioned that New York's Memorial Sloan-Kettering Hospital specialized in Ewing's tumor. I looked the doctor in the eyes and asked, "What would you do?" Without hesitation, he said, "If it were my son, I'd go to New York. I wouldn't want him to have his leg removed if he didn't have to."

So we took Ben right out of there and went on to New York. For most of five years, Memorial Sloan-Kettering Hospital was at the center of our world. Ben fought the cancer courageously. It was a prolonged battle, using every weapon available—surgeries, chemotherapy and radiation, alternative treatments, bonemarrow tests, blood transfusions, and endless injections. Plus massive doses of prayer and every ounce of hope and energy we could muster.

Ben and I made countless trips between Greensboro and New York City, staying during Ben's radiation treatments with Norman's brother Ralph, his wife, Sue, and their children, Jeff and Liz, who lived on Long Island. Ben's tumor was both within and on top of his upper leg bone. The radiation was so intense that the treatments affected the good part of his bone as well as the bad, leaving his leg very weak. The doctors had to insert a metal plate to support the bone where the tumor had been removed, which caused Ben a great deal of pain and problems. The plate was subject to infections, requiring that his leg be opened up periodically to have the plate cleaned and the infection sites repaired.

The radiation essentially eradicated the tumor, but it didn't remove the cancer from Ben's bone marrow or bloodstream. About once a month, Ben and I drove up to New York so that he could have a full day of chemotherapy treatment. If we drove straight back, we got home about one o'clock in the morning. Often we stopped over with our friends Nancy and Herb Clark and their family in Baltimore, a welcome break during the long drives.

Once on our way home, about midnight, we were driving a lonely stretch of interstate in southern Virginia, just north of the North Carolina line. I felt alone. Ben was asleep in the back seat. I hadn't seen another car on the road in a long time, and I was anxious to get home, so I was exceeding the speed limit. I couldn't believe that I got pulled over by the police. I had to drive into a small town where the public officials seemed to have quite a little operation going. They directed me to write out my check to the magistrate who was sitting there. I'm convinced that he pocketed the money. That episode felt like a small injustice added to huge injury.

During Ben's illness, I got in touch with my grief just enough to be angry with Norman for not being with us for this long battle. But most of the time, I just continued my efforts to be brave. I prayed to be half as brave as Ben was.

After his first examination at NIH, Ben had stayed with some of our friends in Baltimore while Bill and I returned to the hospital to get the report. When we got back to our friends' home, Ben was lying on the couch. He cried when we told him that the doctors had confirmed that he had cancer and that they were going to have to amputate his leg. It had come upon him—upon all of us—so suddenly.

But after that, Ben seemed to accept with grace the truth of his life. He was never a complainer. During his illness, friends brought him all sorts of games and puzzles. He put together intricate model airplanes and ships. He never sat idle, never became self-pitying or morose.

One of the hardest struggles for him was accepting the loss of his hair. Young men didn't shave their heads back then, as some do now. Ben bore the deep embarrassment of being a teenager who looked "different." He wore a knit Navy watch cap. Though it didn't happen often, sometimes at school a kid would grab it off his head, leaving him feeling humiliated. But most of the time his peers at New Garden Friends School respected the cap—and Ben.

For periods of time it appeared that his cancer was in remission. At those times, Ben was able to enjoy our family camping and beach trips, and he even took short hikes with us. We were amazed at what he could do. He was on crutches for most of five years. His arms were strong, and he could make those crutches fly up the stairs and over trails. At times his hair even grew back. Although it had been straight before chemo, it came back wavy and thick—a beautiful head of hair.

Bill was tremendously helpful and supportive throughout Ben's illness, but it unavoidably put a strain on our new marriage. And I began to see that I had entered the marriage prematurely, needing more time to grieve Norman's death and begin personal healing. One snowy day, I realized that there was a profound emptiness in my heart, a void that I needed to address.

In the late fall of 1972, Bill and I agreed to separate. I had just begun a new job at the YWCA. Within a few weeks, Dad died unexpectedly of a heart attack, leaving me stunned and bereft. My brother Bill moved in with the children and me, and the care he needed was almost overwhelming at times. Less than a year before, my brother John had suffered a violent death. In 1973, Bill and I divorced. It was a time of seismic loss and change.

Through all the difficulties and demands, I was surrounded and upheld by a circle of close friends. One friendship that especially sustained me during those difficult days had developed a few years after our return to Charlotte in 1967. Bob Welsh was the American Friends Service Committee's Southeast area director of the Volunteers In Service to America (VISA), a Quaker domestic peace corps. He, his wife, Margaret, and their children joined the Charlotte Friends Meeting.

After several years in the Army Reserves, Bob had come to the realization that he could no longer serve in the military. He applied to the draft board for reclassification as a conscientious objector but was turned down. He insisted that on moral grounds he was no longer able to participate in Reserve duties, even if his refusal meant serving time in prison. Eventually a local attorney intervened, and Bob was granted a discharge.

The war in Vietnam continued to escalate. In May 1969, in protest of the bombing of Cambodia by U.S. forces, the American Friends Service Committee called for a national twenty-four-hour fast, followed by a silent vigil at the White House. As a member of the AFSC board of directors, compelled by the war's grinding escalations, I wanted to go. Bill gladly agreed to look after the children. Bob, and a young VISA volunteer named Peter Alexander, and I planned to go to Washington together in our Volkswagen bug.

On the morning of our departure, Bob was waiting on the meetinghouse porch to tell us, regretfully, that he was unable to join us. He thrust into our car window a box of chocolate chip cookies he had made as a small offering for our journey—a simple, touching act of thoughtfulness and generosity. Peter and I, already into our fast, had to fight the urge to dig into those tempting cookies on the long drive.

The silent vigil was an impressive and solemn event, deeply meaningful for me. On the way home, hungry after a long twenty-four hours of consuming nothing but water and juice, we broke into the box of cookies. As I was driving in heavy Washington traffic, I popped one, whole, into my mouth, and smiled. Surely it was the best cookie I had ever eaten. Consuming Bob's simple gift somehow felt like a form of communion with him.

In the summer of 1969, Bob's stint with VISA came to an end. He reentered college teaching, securing a position in the English department at the University of Tennessee in Chattanooga. Saying goodbye to the Welsh family was poignant for Charlotte Friends. We had been moved by the courageous witness of both Bob and Margaret in facing the draft-board challenges, and we cherished their contributions to the life of the Meeting.

Bob and I continued our friendship from a distance, exchanging letters, poems, and thoughts. With his passion for literature, he introduced me to the wonderful Bushman writings of Laurens van der Post and the poetry of Rainer Maria Rilke, both of which I came to treasure. I shared with him my favorite poems by Gerard Manley Hopkins.

Bob possessed a refinement of spirit, a vulnerable sensitivity, and a courageous integrity. As our relationship deepened, we felt like fellow seekers on a high mountain path, heading somewhere we could not yet imagine. I was astonished to have five vivid dreams in succession that included Bob, all of which were characterized by themes of quest and journey.

Eventually, our direction became clearer as both of our marriages suffered and then ended. Although our connection felt unique, it was doubtless not unlike many other relationships that begin as a friendship and, over time, transmute into something deeper, at last leading to a committed love. These words by Rilke in *Letters to a Young Poet* capture the essence of what Bob and I were experiencing together:

> *Love consists in this, that two solitudes*
> *protect and touch and greet each other.*
>
> *The future enters into us, in order to*
> *transform itself in us, long before it happens.*

Bob was of immeasurable help to the children and me during Ben's illness, bringing brightness and joy into an enormously scary and shadowed time. What was opening up between us kept me going and gave me strength. It was like a beacon light in a dark and turbulent sea.

During the summer of 1974, the doctors gave us grave news: only one hope remained to save Ben's life, and it involved daily treatments at Sloan-Kettering. Faced with that challenging truth, we knew we had to get Ben closer to the hospital. We decided that the children and I would move to New York, and Bob would come up and visit on weekends when he could. We found a nice house to rent in Setauket, on Long Island, close to Ralph and Sue and the children, which was owned by the widow of an actor who had played Tarzan in the movies. Rope swings hung in the back yard. When they came over, the owner's children still played "Tarzan," even though their daddy had died. My kids found it funny to be living in the home of the Tarzan family— one rare and unexpected source of delight in those very bleak days.

The house was almost two hours from New York City. Every weekday morning that fall and winter, I got up before dawn to get Tina, almost fourteen, and Emily, who was ten, off to school. Everything was upset in the girls' lives, and they hated the schools they attended. They just wanted to be with Ben and me. We got two kittens, Ping and Pong, to provide a little comfort and entertainment. We survived that year with the help of Pepto-Bismol, a necessary part of breakfast to get the girls through the day. As soon as they were on the school bus, Ben and I got in the car and made the long trek into the city for his chemo treatments, hoping that we wouldn't get stuck in another Long Island Expressway traffic jam.

Bless his heart, Bob came up about every other weekend—all that way in an old jalopy; I can't even remember what kind of clunker we had then. His frequent visits with us were a lifesaver. On October 5, 1974, Bob and I got married in the yard of the Setauket house in an informal, Quaker-style wedding.

Ben looked cheerful but frail in our wedding snapshots. Despite daily chemotherapy and our continued prayers, he was growing weaker and weaker. When we went back to Greensboro for Christmas, Ben's blood counts dipped so low that we had to take him to the hospital for blood transfusions. He was growing weary of the agonizing regimen necessary for survival. He told a family friend that he just didn't have much more to give to his struggle to live.

Still, we tried to be hopeful. The kids and I went back to Long Island after the holidays. In February, Ben's doctor told us that Ben would have to be admitted to the hospital as an in-patient. Emily and Tina moved in with Ralph, Sue, and their children. I took Ben into the hospital and stayed with our friends Peggy and Allan Brick in Englewood, New Jersey, on the edge of New York City. I went to the hospital and stayed with Ben every day, seeing the girls on weekends.

After a while, it was too hard for Emily, who decided that she wanted to go home to Greensboro. When Bob made a visit in March, she went back with him and reentered Friends School. Tina stayed on with Ralph and Sue and their family, taking the train into New York City on the weekends to be with Ben and me.

The Bricks were wonderful friends during a terribly difficult time. Their home was where I learned to drink strong Medaglia D'oro coffee. As usual, I was trying to hold too much together and keeping all my emotions to myself. Allan encouraged me to participate in a counseling group with him, which was a help.

Several roommates revolved through Ben's life during his stay at the hospital. Thomas, who at sixteen was just slightly older than Ben, had leukemia. He was a wonderful young man, and Ben enjoyed him so much. He was a lot like Ben—sensitive, intelligent, good-spirited. One evening the nurses came and took Ben hastily out of the room. I had seen the inevitable coming several hours before it happened, and it broke my heart. Thomas's death was very hard on Ben, and on me as well. I was moved to write a poem of tribute to Thomas.

The oncology ward was filled with stories of valor. It seemed that kids with cancer had been given special dispensations of love, wisdom, and grace. And fortitude. I met one little boy from Israel, whose mother could barely speak English. She came every day and went to the small kitchen on the hospital ward and cooked Middle Eastern dishes for her son. But I knew that he wasn't going to make it.

As time went on, Ben seemed to have a deepening spiritual experience. He didn't talk about it much, but I believe that he had an understanding of eternity. I never felt any fear in him. He was stoic, like Dad, keeping a lot to himself. Resilient and strong of heart, he looked for the brightness in any situation. He had been very hopeful when we started the treatments in New York. I think that until sometime in the last year of his life, he believed that he was going to be cured. I think we all did.

But when spring came and Ben grew weaker, he began to give up. I too started to feel that we were going to lose him. My heart was so low that I didn't have the strength to do more than get myself to Ben's hospital bedside each morning and stay with him until late evening. I began to give up hope for a miracle. I could neither imagine his future nor the lack of it. I could not accept what was becoming inevitable.

Ben's final weeks were so tough and challenging, both physically and emotionally, his condition and suffering so unspeakably sad, it is almost too much to recall, much less describe. But, even in that sorrowful and excruciating time, we managed to celebrate Ben's sixteenth birthday on May 12. Confined to his bed, he was very weak, but not too weak to blow out the candles on the cake we brought to him. Some of the nurses dropped by to wish him a happy birthday, to lighten things up a bit.

Bill Beidler came to New York to see him at the end. Ben loved Bill and had always looked up to him, and Bill returned his love fully. Bill was a genius with equipment and technical things, and after our divorce, Ben often went over to our old house after school to work on mechanical projects with Bill in his basement workshop. The two of them repaired appliances and cars and built a radio together, and they had grown close. Bill saw Ben in the hospital on a Saturday, then joined us that night at the Bricks' home.

Bob, the girls, and I planned to go see Ben on Sunday morning, and we assumed that Bill would go with us. But he decided to leave for home that morning, right after breakfast. Maybe Bill, who always tried to keep his emotions under lock and key, knew that Ben was going to die, and he just couldn't bear to go back. He would never, never have intentionally hurt Ben; in his own way, maybe he believed that he was protecting not only his own feelings, but also Ben's.

When we got to the hospital that morning, Ben asked where Bill was. When I told him that Bill had to go on back home, Ben burst out in sobs. The nurse asked him what was wrong. Ben choked through his tears, "My father left me and didn't say goodbye."

The nurses on the pediatric oncology ward were wonderful. Some were veterans. One or two had been there during the entire five years of our relationship with the hospital, and probably long before we came on the scene. One day I said to my favorite nurse, the oldest, "There is so much sadness here, how can you nurses keep going?"

She said to me, "We learn a lot from the patients. We learn a lot about life, about its unpredictability. There have been children in here, I wouldn't give you a dime for their chances to have a future. But I'd see them two or three years later, and they'd be in remission, they'd be OK. I never write anybody off. That kind of hope keeps me going."

A favorite of Ben's was the doctor in charge of radiology. He had a wonderful spirit and a good relationship with Ben. Toward the end of our time at Sloan-Kettering, I learned that he himself had contracted cancer and died. That was difficult to hear; he had been so good to Ben.

The only person on the staff I didn't care for was the social worker for the ward. My general inclination is to like people, but I couldn't make it work with her. She was always saying the wrong thing. She was young, and I know she was doing her best, but she should have been in an entirely different line of work. She always came so cheery into a room that was reeling with pain. She appeared in Ben's room shortly before Memorial Day, and said brightly, "Well, what are you all going to do for the holiday?" I thought, "You know, my son is dying—and you're talking about a holiday?" But I just said, "We're going to stay right here."

After she left, Ben asked, "Do you all have any plans for Chautauqua this summer?" Grandma Hazel was still there, and all of us went to Chautauqua in the summers, even during Ben's illness. The way he asked the question made me realize that he knew he wasn't going with us this time. So I said, "No, we don't have any plans. We're just going to stay here."

Ben knew the end was near. He was always wise. At the age of sixteen, he seemed to me like an "old soul." I think he was prepared.

Toward the end, Ben was in a room by himself. He had a night nurse who was a young man, with curly, red hair. I wish I could remember his name. He let me know that he and Ben had shared some good talks late at night. I have a great admiration for nurses, because they have such power to minister to people— not only to their bodies, but also to their hearts and souls. I was comforted to know that Ben and this nurse could talk in a way that Ben and I couldn't.

One Saturday, Allan Brick encouraged me to go to an all-day workshop. I hated to be away from Ben for a whole day, but I went, and I was grateful that I did. At the end of the day, the facilitators asked all the participants—no matter what the quality of their voice—to stand up and sing a song. I've always loved to sing for fun, but I'm shy about it, because I don't have a good voice. I was preoccupied with thoughts of Ben. I don't know precisely where the song came from, but I stood up and made my way through an old English ballad, "He's Gone Away."

And then he went away. My first child and only son lost his battle to live on May 25, 1975. It was a Sunday, just before Memorial Day, less than two weeks after his sixteenth birthday. We were all there. Emily was too young to be allowed on the ward, so she waited downstairs in the hospital lobby. Bob went back and forth, staying with her for a while and then coming back up to be with us in Ben's room.

On that last morning, a lovely young woman was singing in the hall near Ben's room. We had met her several weeks before. She played her guitar and sang for what seemed to be the love of it, and the love in her heart. She was a volunteer at the hospital, in training as a music therapist, a troubadour of cheer. She had the sweetest, most consoling voice, and a warm, peaceful smile. She often sang to patients on the pediatrics floor and to their families in the hall and waiting rooms. We took to her easily and looked forward to hearing her sing.

On that last morning of Ben's life, she gently invited herself into the room where we were gathered around his bed. She sat a little distance away and asked for Ben's favorite songs. The only ones I could remember at that moment were the Beatles' "Here Comes the Sun" and "Michael, Row Your Boat Ashore." Ben loved those songs, so she quietly played and sang those songs of hope for our boy whose hope was fast slipping away. Then she left without a word, just a smile to acknowledge our thanks. I will never forget that moment, the irony and poignancy of it. To this day I cannot listen to "Here Comes the Sun" without tears welling up from my heart.

Just before the end, in the final minutes of his life in that hospital room, a deep, suppressed anger that had been inside Ben burst out. His body was falling apart, but there was still breath

in his lungs enough for him to vehemently protest. He wailed—
the first and only time I ever heard him utter these words—"It's
not fair. It's just not fair!" All I could do was love him and hold
him and agree. I told my dear, brave son, "That's right, Ben,
that's right, it's not fair. But we're with you. We're right here."
He began gasping for air. I was encouraging him to let go, when
what I wanted more than anything was to hold and keep him
forever. A nurse gave him some medication to relax him. We did
all we could to comfort him until he took his last, labored
breath.

We stayed with his body for a while. Several of the doctors
who had been treating Ben over the years came in. They expressed their condolences to us. And then one requested permission for an autopsy. When I asked why, he answered, "In the
interest of science. It's not to discover why. We know what he
died of."

I didn't want an autopsy. Ben's body had suffered such assault,
I didn't want anything else done to it. I just wanted it to be over.
I wanted the doctors to leave, but a few of them kept insisting.
One said, "Ben lived an extraordinarily long time for someone
with that kind of cancer, and we thought if we did an autopsy,
we might discover why." I looked him in the eyes and told him,
"I don't know why he lived as long as he did, but you won't
discover it through an autopsy." Then Bob said firmly to the
doctors, "The answer is no."

Ben was right, in the anguish and anger of his final moments,
to name the unfairness of his suffering and death. I had grown
up believing in a fair and reasonable world. But my trust in such
a world was shattered again by Ben's death, as it had been by
Norman's.

After Ben died, Bob, the girls, and I went back to Greensboro.
Though I was glad to be home, for several months—maybe the
better part of a year—my head and heart were still in New York
at that hospital. I wanted to go back. I wanted Ben to be alive.
It's not that I wished for that long night of illness to continue,
but I found myself dreaming and thinking about being back on

that floor at the hospital. It had been our home, Ben's and mine, for so long.

After Ben died, I wanted to die too. Life felt devoid of meaning. I felt that I had lost God, or that God had lost me. Back then, every time I took a shower, I cried. I didn't want to be weeping all the time around Bob, Tina, and Emily, and the shower was the safest place to mourn. The pain just kept leaking out.

I learned then that if you want to get your heart open, sing old hymns—or watch *The Waltons*. It helped me immensely to dig into memory and sing to myself the hymns from my early Methodist days, which evoked deep emotion. And I cried every week when TV's Walton family said their goodnights to one another at the end of each episode. Tina and Emily always teased me good-naturedly about it. I was slowly letting out my feelings, discovering my heart.

Looking back on those days, I realize that I was crying for Norman, too. And for many other losses. By that time, Dad had died, Mother had died, and my brother John had died. My husband had died. And now my son had died.

I did some work with peer counseling and stumbled into a deep pit of fear and grief. I joined a bereavement group with other mothers and fathers who had lost children, which was extremely helpful. But I found it so hard to be around friends who had children Ben's age, especially boys—to see mothers with sons growing up. I was envious and sad for a very long time. It's hard to outlive your children. There's something not right about that, about having a child who doesn't grow up. You want your children to grow up.

But I continued to be grateful for the graces in our hospital experience, Ben's and mine. Two years after his death, I enrolled in the graduate program in health education at the University of North Carolina in Greensboro. I conducted the research for my master's thesis at Bowman Gray School of Medicine and Baptist Hospital. Being in a hospital was comforting and familiar. Common sense might have dictated that I close that door and stay as far away as possible from a hospital. But I knew that in the midst of the pain and the death, there was life there. An awful lot of life. And courage, and love.

When I look back on Ben's illness and death, I also feel in my heart how much Tina and Emily suffered. I was so riveted on helping Ben survive that it was difficult to give my daughters the attention they deserved. I wandered in a period of darkness and mourning for a long time afterward. But eventually, all the crying and the grief work helped me to turn and see my daughters more clearly, to be more present to them. And to feel deep gratitude, great tenderness, and immense love for them.

Ben's death was difficult for each of them in a different way. Emily was the little sister who was always running to catch up with her older siblings. She would mess up their playthings and little games, not meaning to. Ben and Emily were often in a bit of contention. When he died, she lost her brother before she had truly found him. There was something between Ben and Emily that was waiting to bloom, that never had a chance.

Ben and Tina grew through childhood together. She was fourteen and a half when Ben left us. That was an impressionable time; she was just heading into the teenage years in a big way. I think that she was just lost for a while after he died. The first night back in Greensboro, Tina wandered through the house, unable to sleep. She didn't want to be back in that home so void of her beloved brother, but she didn't know where else to be. She came into my room and told me she didn't know where to sleep. Both girls really needed a brother, and they didn't have one after that.

For a while after Ben died—for a few years—I felt his presence with me, as I have felt Norman's presence from time to time over the years. And then, with Ben, I remember one day feeling a shift, an awareness that his spirit was no longer near in the same way. It was very palpable, as though his spirit had moved on to another realm. It wasn't that I couldn't reach him, but he just wasn't as close anymore.

Although Ben died a long time ago, whenever I hear Bach's beautiful hymn "Sheep May Safely Graze," I think of a particular day in the last year of his life, when we were living on Long Island. An older teacher of homebound children—a teddy bear of a guy—visited Ben each week. At the time, we were still holding onto the frail hope that Ben would someday regain his health and return to school.

One day while Ben's teacher was there, the opening strains of "Sheep May Safely Graze" came on the radio. The teacher stopped in mid-sentence and invited us all to listen. It was a favorite of his. The hymn had a powerful effect on me. I was watching my son slip away from us and from life. At that moment, the words of the song felt bitterly ironic. Yes, I thought, sheep may safely graze, knowing a caring shepherd is watching over them. But is Ben safe in the hands of the Good Shepherd? Can he recover and live?

The answer was both no and yes. Ben did not recover, but he was still in the hands of the Good Shepherd. Throughout the five years after his diagnosis, he endured his suffering in the midst of a circle of love, of family and friends—divine and angelic, as well as human. Ben knew, I believe, that he was in a mighty keep of love, the kind about which Bach wrote. This assurance undergirded the bravery, stoicism, and nobility of spirit with which he bore his pain and tragedy. He once remarked that he was glad it was he who was enduring the pain instead of his sisters.

Accepting Ben's death was the hardest task of my life. I, too, had to contend with my anger and with my belief in a loving God. To this day, the suffering of children is almost unbearable to me. Nothing about it is fair. But Ben bore the unfairness, the darkness and horror, like the great soldier that he was. I inscribed on his gravestone one word: *Courage.*

It is so hard to write about someone as close as one's child, to try to do justice to a life that was so much a part of my own—someone who was always inside my heart. I think most mothers would say that we love our children all the same, but we have a different relationship and chemistry with each one.

Ben and I were cut out from the same cloth. He resembled my side of the family, with Mother's wide, full lips and large, dark, expressive eyes. Ben and I often knew what the other was thinking. We understood each other on an intuitive, almost visceral, level. He seemed to be aware of my feelings and moods. Though we couldn't always talk about the most important things, we understood.

Even today I cannot speak about or even think of my son without a catch in my throat, without love and gratitude for who he was and, I believe, still is. And here there is real comfort—that he is, finally, completely safe within the folds of the Good Shepherd, where mercy, peace, and joy abound, and within the arms of his dad, who loved him so.

Anne and a serious Ben, about 10.

Anne with Ben, Emily, and Christina.

During our 1999 visit, Christina, Anne, and Emily in the back row receive a welcome at a primary school in My Lai.

Emily planting a tree at the My Lai Primary School.

Christina, Anne, and former Prime Minister Pham Van Dong.

Emily, Christina, and I receive flowers at a memorial celebration of Norman at the Peace Park north of Hanoi

Anne, our translator, and To Huu, poet laureate and author of the poem "Emily, My Child."

Emily and Christina.

Alan Marler

5

Lighting the Horizon

Our voices of protest have till now been little more than a whisper. I hope that Norman Morrison's protest demonstration will rouse the conscience of Americans so that the whisper will become a roar.
—A SUPPORTER FROM
HASTINGS ON HUDSON, NEW YORK

*A*t noon on a Friday in May 1980, an unexpected visitor walked onto Hazel Morrison's porch in Chautauqua and knocked on the front door. The young man explained to Norman's mother that he had served in the Air Force in Vietnam and had turned against the war. He said he wanted to talk about her son and his sacrificial protest.

Brian Willson was a graduate of Chautauqua High School. His parents lived in nearby Ashville, New York. Though Hazel was initially a little dubious about inviting a stranger into the house, she was moved by his earnestness. Brian stayed for about an hour, sharing his story and learning more about Norman's.

In 1969, Brian Willson had led a combat security unit in Vietnam that provided protection at South Vietnamese and U.S. airbases. He and his comrades were exposed to regular attacks, especially at night, from mortars and rifle fire. His duties included accompanying a Vietnamese lieutenant to assess the success of bombing missions against villages that had been targeted for their alleged sympathy with the enemy. Just a month after Brian arrived, he witnessed the destruction of the village of Sa Dec:

With smoldering ruins throughout, the ground was strewn with bodies of villagers and their farm animals, many of whom were motionless and bloody, murdered from bomb shrapnel and napalm. Several were trying to get up on their feet, and others were moving ever so slightly as they cried and moaned. Most of the victims I witnessed were women and children. At one dramatic moment, I encountered at close range a young wounded woman lying on the ground clutching three young disfigured children. I stared, aghast, at the woman's open eyes. Upon closer examination, I discovered that she, and what I presumed were her children, all were dead, but napalm had melted much of the woman's facial skin, including her eyelids. As the Vietnamese lieutenant and I silently made the one-plus hour return trip to our airbase in my jeep, I knew that my life was never going to be the same again.

Brian, who felt that he was "struggling for physical and psychic survival" during the war, began expressing his opposition to the bombing campaigns and their devastation. After five months in Vietnam, he was removed from his unit and sent home early. He completed law school and worked for several years on research and educational efforts related to veterans' issues, including posttraumatic stress disorder, Agent Orange poisoning, homelessness, suicide, alcoholism, and drug abuse.

In January 1986, Brian traveled to Nicaragua and again observed firsthand the devastations of aggressive U.S. foreign policy on a civilian population. Supported by the Reagan administration, funded by the U.S. Congress, and trained by the CIA, Contra forces were terrorizing and murdering Nicaraguans, particularly in the country's vulnerable border areas. Gunfire punctuated the days and red tracers lit up the nights at three agricultural cooperatives in the northern mountains that were under attack while Brian visited. "I witnessed the caravan of open caskets on horse-drawn wagons carrying eleven dead civilians from those attacks, mostly women and children," Brian recorded. "I mumbled under my breath, 'I have been here before.' . . . I wept openly, almost uncontrollably, along the roadside near the cemetery."

Brian Willson had a revelation that day. "Vietnam was not an aberration," he wrote. "Neither was Nicaragua. Nor the original Holocaust of Native Americans, nor the subsequent Holocaust of kidnapped Africans. Nor U.S. interventions and murders in countless other locations over time and regions."

Over the years, Brian participated in several fasts and acts of nonviolent civil disobedience to draw attention to U.S. policy. Most notable was a demonstration at the Concord Naval Weapons Station in California in 1987. Protesting U.S. weapons shipments to Nicaragua and El Salvador, he and two other members of a Veterans Peace Action Team sat on the railroad tracks to block a train entering the station. Though the protestors' presence was well publicized and highly visible, the train crew had been given orders not to stop, and Brian was run over. He suffered a severe skull fracture and multiple other wounds, losing both his legs below the knees.

That traumatic incident anchors his autobiography, *On Third World Legs*, published in 1992. The book also recounts the story Brian shared with Hazel on her porch, an account of a visit with a South Vietnamese family during the war in late May 1969. One of the family's members worked at the airbase library and had taken note of the books Brian borrowed, concluding that he disagreed with the war. Over dinner in the family's home, they together lamented the destruction being unleashed on Vietnam by the United States.

After the meal, the family offered songs, accompanied by a variety of musical instruments. One they translated into English especially for Brian. They dedicated it to Norman, the subject of the song:

> *The flame which burned you will clear and lighten*
> *   life*
> *And many new generations of people will find the*
> *   horizon,*

> *Then a day will come when the American people*
> *Will rise, one after another, for life.*

Brian Willson was stunned by the song. He wrote in his autobiography that Norman's sacrifice "had had very little impact on me. . . . It did not register for a while that this was the same Norman Morrison who had also graduated from Chautauqua High School, and had been the first Eagle Scout I ever knew. I thought in 1965 that what Norman did was a foolish act, and felt sorry that Norman had cracked, and shamed himself."

In that Vietnamese home three-and-a-half years later, in the presence of a compassionate family that shared his outrage over the war, Brian broke into tears. He was, he wrote, "trembling with emotions in the midst of some kind of metaphysical, spiritual experience, for the first time sensing a profound connection with Norman"—a connection, he says, that has remained.

When his autobiography was published, Brian Willson sent me a copy. Penned in it was this message: "To Anne—Thanks for your presence on the planet. Know that you, Norman, and your children have had an impact on me that transcends any easy expression. This brief book is one attempt to describe how your influence, among others, has contributed to my moccasins, to my steps on the trail toward sacredness." The dedication page of his autobiography carries these words: "This book is dedicated to Norman Morrison whose ultimate expression of conscience and anguish helped light the horizon so that I could see."

I was deeply moved by Brian's words and actions. In those painful years following Ben's death, as I grieved the loss of Norman more deeply, I found comfort and hope knowing that the fire Norman had lit was seen by others, like Brian Willson, as a beacon of light.

I was thankful for several enduring tributes to Norman. In 1966 the Royal Shakespeare Company, under the direction of Peter Brooke, had staged a musical by Adrian Mitchell called *US* in London's Aldwych Theatre. Inspired by Norman's sacrifice and including a reenactment of his death, the production was sharply critical of the U.S. role in the Vietnam War.

In 1968, Felix Greene, an American writer living in London, sent me a copy of a literary journal published in Budapest, Hungary. Its pages contained photographs of several bronze sculptures by Farkas Aladar on the theme of Vietnam. Among them was a moving statue in honor of Norman and dedicated to me. The male figure, in an anguished, heroic stance, holds a child in his outstretched right arm. In his left hand he holds high a cross.

Because Norman's sacrifice was in the realm of spirit and intuition rather than reason, perhaps poets were most easily able to grasp it. One poet called Norman "Prometheus at the Pentagon," an allusion to the god of mythology who brought fire to humankind and was known for his boldness, sympathy, and willingness to suffer pain for the sake of others. Several used imagery of a phoenix rising out of ashes, calling to mind the visionary mythical bird that set itself on fire and died to make room for new life—a symbol of rebirth, resurrection, and immortality.

Using Pentecost imagery, poet David Ferguson wrote that Norman "spoke in a tongue of flame." Amy Clampitt described "the extravaganza of a man afire having seized, tigerlike, the attention it now holds with the tenacity of napalm." Errol Hess asked, "Emily, did you see flowers as the match lit, as fire exploded from your father's fuel-soaked clothes, burning like a fast wick to light my conscience?"

A few of the poems have been particularly moving and meaningful to me:

Norman Morrison

On November 2 1965
in the multi-colored multi-minded
United beautiful states of terrible America
Norman Morrison set himself on fire
outside the Pentagon. . . .
He did it in Washington where everyone
could see
because
people were being set on fire

in the dark corners of Vietnam where nobody
could see. . . .
He simply burned away his clothes,
his passport, his pink-tinted skin,
put on a new skin of flame
and became
Vietnamese.
—ADRIAN MITCHELL

To Norman Morrison

He lit a flame.
And round the campfires of the world
We sat and stared.
The crazy dance of life and death
Flicked there before us.
How could the noble blaze
Of this man's life
Burn thus so bright
And yet consume itself?

He lit a flame.
He struck a match
Upon the unbearable abrasions
Of sufferings half a world away
Within his tendered heart.
The purifying fire
Then cleansed away
The dross of indecision;
Forever fused were
Thought and act,
Spirit and flesh,
Inseparable.

He lit a flame.
The winds of curiosity

Caught the spark
And blew it carelessly.
Yet wherever there was a man
Who ever wondered what it was
To be a man
It lit another flame.
The torch of life
Was thus passed on
In self-consuming passion.

He lit a flame.
And round the campfires of the world
He dances in our eyes.

—JAMES BOND

Hugh Ogden, a poet and English professor at Trinity College in Hartford, Connecticut, who died tragically in 2006, was a childhood friend of Norman's. In 1990 he wrote a long elegy to Norman, anchored in his memories of a Holy Land replica that had been set up at Chautauqua and their sailing adventures there:

Chautauqua

I.

One thing to sing for a soldier or lover,
another for you who helped quicken me to
life,
walked the miniature valleys of Palestine at
Chautauqua
and made Judea real.
Once we walked that replica
and went from the Dead Sea up to Galilee
in fifteen minutes.
You, a twelve-year old in a shirt and tie,
naming the dahlias on the western border,

and in the middle,
Nazareth, Jerusalem.
The Jordan flowed a two-foot wide stream
of blue and a single bridge over it.
Warm air trickled.
Years later, the American government sent
troops to Vietnam
and the world looked at you in the
newspaper.
And I had a friend and he will always be
slightly older
and go down from Jerusalem in the foliage of
Siloam's pool,
the flux of the gardens.
Around him children will gather
and leaves, what the air renders of summer,
what the wind.

II.
I listen to some obscure mixing of history and
memory.
The mainsail billows with the wind
from over the tiny hills and valleys of
Palestine
and The Lightning heels over so far
I'm frightened the boat will founder.
Johnson sends Marines to Da Nang.
You reach down and set the Nazareth sign
back upright, kick sand from the path.
Dean Rusk holds a news conference.
I buy a newspaper on the steps of the Union
in Ann Arbor,
light blowing November snow.
For days afterwards
your picture appears on classroom walls,
as everyone talks about how you drove

to Washington with your year-old daughter,
went to the river entrance of the Pentagon
and stood in the stream of office-workers
ending their day.
At Chautauqua you conjure Bible stories
from the charred wood of a camp fire,
dream of attending seminary to understand
Jesus,
rush back from the lake to be with your
mother
in late afternoon.
How the hands of others flutter over
a young child's head!
How you would write in the sand with your
finger
or sit there and recall the book of John.
See, how I know still the story of men
who could not see how a blind man washed
his eyes
and came back seeing.
He came back seeing though born blind.
I see you in white shirt and loose tie
walking the bridge over Jordan.
I see you sponging water from the bilge
as we return to the buoy,
calmly holding the mooring cleat
as I try to tie a bowline.
I see you in a meetinghouse
speaking without raising your arms.
I see you sitting on the grass outside an
amphitheater
listening to Bach's B Minor Mass,
your eyes oblivious to the brown bats that flit
from the roof.
I see you getting out of an old Cadillac in the
Pentagon parking lot.

You wrap your daughter in a plaid blanket,
then carry her under one arm,
a gallon jug hung from the other.
No one stops to speak,
the river tinged gray eastward, slough time,
slow,
then fast, windows alight in the squat cement
building.
You climb up the parapet, stalks of crimson
weed-flower
isolated on the brown-green grass.
She cuddles against your sweater,
reaches a fist to your chin.
You put her down, take a few steps,
put the jug over your head and pour.
She smiles at the flame, kicks off the blanket.
Gaps in the clouds above, splinterings of
flame,
coughing.
A colonel runs up and throws you to the
ground.
She cries.
A woman picks her up and sways.
You struggle to your feet, cup your right hand
over your ear,
your other a flame above.
In the Potomac brown weed, bits of
cardboard.
White sheared wind over Chautauqua Lake
burns against the mainsail.
Hundreds of people crowd the parking lot,
the cement walkway.
You lie curled with your head almost touching
your corduroys.
She stares up at a stranger in dusk
as all Washington lights up the river.

III.
If I had known,
pulling the mainsail taut because you asked,
I would have pulled myself closer,
touched your hand.
I would have asked why
you would bring your daughter to
Washington
in a distant November.
I would like to believe you had her with you
because
that was one of the days you took care of her.
As you drive by the refineries flaring gas near
Baltimore
you suddenly needed to go to the Pentagon
with her in the baby seat beside you.
You forgot how a child gazes up at an adult.
Oblivious and wild for peace.
You breathed close to murder
and then put her aside to change our history.
Now, twenty-five years later,
I lay down here the only truth I know,
these words you speak:
I wanted so much.
I wanted to stand against my country when
it brought a gun to a child's head.
My child watched me burn myself by the
Potomac.
I wanted to brush and brush again
her hair and give her a home,
a full pleated dress with a white sash,
a just community.
I wanted her to be able to walk to school
unafraid
and have friends and play with dolls
in an open living room.

I wanted her breasts to grow firm, grow round,
her wide eyes startle even me.
I wanted the winds off Chautauqua forever
and over again,
for her to put up sail and strike it,
the reach of a light breeze carrying her to the
buoy,
for her to go to the miniature replica of
Palestine
with children and stand by the Jordan
and go down in the foliage to the path
where a blind man washed clay from his eyes
and saw
because he believed.

—HUGH OGDEN

A few of the poems written in the wake of Norman's death directly addressed then Secretary of Defense Robert McNamara, near whose window at the Pentagon Norman burned himself:

Of Late

"Stephen Smith, University of Iowa
sophomore,
burned what he said was his draft card"
and Norman Morrison, Quaker,
of Baltimore Maryland,
burned what he said was himself.
You Robert McNamara, burned what you
said was
a concentration of the Enemy Aggressor.
No news medium troubled to put it in quotes.

And Norman Morrison, Quaker,
of Baltimore Maryland,
burned what he said was himself.

He said it with simple materials such as
would be found in your kitchen.

In your office you were informed.
Reporters got cracking frantically on the
mental disturbance angle.

So far nothing turns up.
Norman Morrison, Quaker,
of Baltimore Maryland,
burned and while burning, screamed.
No tip-off. No release.
Nothing to quote, to manage to put into
quotes.
Pity the unaccustomed hesitance of the
newspaper editorialists.
Pity the press photographers, not called.

Norman Morrison, Quaker,
of Baltimore Maryland,
burned and was burned and said all that there
is to say in that language.
Twice what is said in yours.
It is a strange sect, Mr. McNamara, under
advice to try
the whole of a thought in silence, and to
oneself.
—GEORGE STARBUCK

Norman R. Morrison 1934–1965

Mr. Secretary, you were looking another way
when grief stalked to your window to forgive
you.
(Harden our hearts enough, and we'll make
the world

*safe for such brutes as we are all becoming
under your guidance.)*

*Yet at the cruel edge
of your five-faced cathedral of violence,
the church of the spirit is ever being rebuilt.*

*In the power and authority of personal life,
because you would not wear your guilt, he
wore it,
companioned to the last by innocence,
the gentle Quaker in your shirt of fire.*
—ALEXANDER LAING

One Quaker was intrepid enough to carry a message directly to McNamara. On the first anniversary of Norman's death, Dorothy Mock of Brevard, North Carolina, walked into the Pentagon, past a guard, up two floors, and through a doorway labeled Secretary of Defense. She had in her hands a bouquet of "fire-burst" chrysanthemums and a letter:

Dear Secretary McNamara:

One year ago . . . Norman Morrison died outside the windows of your office. . . . Generally, public reaction was, "How could a man in his right mind burn himself alive?" and efforts were made to forget him as soon as possible. But some of us cannot forget him. His penitential act, his redemptive suffering for all God's children, haunts us still. For his act was addressed to you, and to all of us, saying, "How can we, in our right minds, burn our brothers—men, women, and innocent children—as we are doing, day after day in Vietnam?" . . .

I feel sure that, if forgiveness be required for what he did, Norman Morrison is the first to be forgiven before Almighty God. But I cannot be so sure that we can ever be forgiven for waging this unthinkable war, paying for it, and allowing it to grow larger and more terrible with each pass-ing day.

Tonight I will join the Friends in Norman Morrison's Meeting in Baltimore in a meeting in his memory, a meet-ing of prayer and intercession, of pleading for a light suf-ficient to penetrate the darkness through which we are groping. You and our President will be uppermost in our prayers.

> *Yours truly,*
> *Dorothy J. Mock*

Dorothy left the letter and a flower with Secretary McNamara's receptionist, who thanked her. Outside, a security guard took her name. A man with a Polaroid camera, claiming he was from the Pentagon's news service, took her picture. She kept a vigil by the River Entrance with a few other Quakers until night fell, and then drove to Baltimore.

Dorothy spent that night in our home. The next morning we shared breakfast. It included apple cider that Norman had made, the weekend before he died, in a treasured old cider press that had belonged to his grandfather. The children and I had helped to gather the apples, and I had canned the cider. Dorothy wrote later, "For me, Norman Morrison is like a Lourdes shrine, from which I gain healing and strength for the tasks that await the living."

I didn't know until thirty years after the fact the impact that Norman's sacrifice had on Robert McNamara. In his 1995 mem-oir, *In Retrospect: The Tragedy and Lessons of Vietnam*, McNamara wrote of the mid-1960s:

> *Antiwar protest had been sporadic and limited up to this time and had not compelled attention. Then came the af-ternoon of November 2, 1965. At twilight that day, a young Quaker named Norman R. Morrison, father of three and an officer of the Stoney [sic] Run Friends Meeting in*

Baltimore, burned himself to death within forty feet of my
Pentagon window. . . .
　Morrison's death was a tragedy not only for his family
but also for me and the country. It was an outcry against
the killing that was destroying the lives of so many Viet-
namese and American youth. . . .
　I reacted to the horror of his action by bottling up my
emotions and avoided talking about them with anyone—
even with my family. I knew Marg and our three children
shared many of Morrison's feelings about the war. . . . And
I believed I understood and shared some of his thoughts.
. . . The episode created tension at home that only deepened
as dissent and criticism of the war continued to grow.

In the Oscar-winning biographical documentary *The Fog of War*, McNamara's voice cracks when he talks about Norman's self-immolation. Columnist Art Buchwald wrote of McNamara that observing Norman's sacrifice was "one of the darkest moments of his life." In his 1996 book *The Living and the Dead: Robert McNamara and Five Lives of a Lost War*, *Washington Post* journalist Paul Hendrickson included Norman among the five individuals who had a deep impact on the Secretary of Defense. "In some ways he may have been correct," McNamara reflected years later on Norman's self-immolation, according to Hendrickson, "if by such actions he could bring to bear the attention he sought."

Hendrickson's book, a finalist for a National Book Award, recounts McNamara's testimony at the *Westmoreland v. CBS* trial. Gen. William Westmoreland, who served as commander of U.S. forces in Vietnam from 1964 to 1968, filed a lawsuit against CBS in 1984. He accused the network of libel for allegations aired in a documentary that he and others had deliberately understated North Vietnam's troop strength in order to maintain U.S. troop morale and domestic support for the war.

In response to a question from the attorney for CBS about when McNamara reached the conclusion that the war could not be won militarily, McNamara responded, "I believe I may have reached it as early as the latter part of 1965." According to Chester L. Cooper's *The Lost Crusade*, observers of McNamara noticed "a discernible change in mood in late 1965. It was not so much a transition from 'hawk' to 'dove.' . . . It was rather a change from overflowing confidence to grave doubts." According to Hendrickson, declassified documents show that within a month of Norman's death, McNamara was "urging the president in memos and in White House meetings and private conversations to consider a bombing pause."

Though McNamara had made similar suggestions to President Johnson before, the late-1965 memos exposed an increased urgency. Taken along with notes of key meetings and transcripts of conversations, these memos, according to Hendrickson, "unmistakably reveal the beginning of the shattering." Norman's self-immolation, he wrote, was "the emotional catalyst for the secret turn."

Though McNamara and others in the Johnson administration continued to escalate the war, which ground on mercilessly for another decade, they did so with deep misgivings. Before his memoir *In Retrospect* was published, in a 1992 article in *Newsweek*, McNamara listed four people or events that had had an impact on his questioning of the war. One—obviously Norman—he identified then only as "a young Quaker." After reading the article, I wrote him a letter:

> *Dear Robert McNamara,*
>
> *I read with great interest your article of August 3, 1992 in* Newsweek. *Thank you for writing it. What you said, I am sure, took courage.*
>
> *The "young Quaker" you referred to in the article was my husband, Norman Morrison. I am writing to let you know his name. I thought you might want to know a little bit about him.*
>
> *He was a gentle person, a Quaker pacifist and a committed Christian; a graduate of divinity school. He was a*

*lover of the Bible, Emerson, and Kierkegaard. A passion-
ate man, he cared deeply about peace and the ideals of this
country. The horror of what America was doing in Vietnam, especially to the innocents, drove him to his desperate act. That, plus a kind of ultimate calling.*

   *I doubt if Norman knew he was within view of your
office window at the Pentagon. But since I did not know
of his plans, I cannot say for sure. As horrible as witness-
ing his self-immolation must have been, perhaps destiny
intended that you should have been that close.*

   *I am sure that Norman would be grateful for your ar-
ticle, your perspectives on the war now, and your work for
world betterment.*

   Thank you again.
   God bless you,
   Anne Morrison Welsh

I received no response to my letter. Until it began to make
headline news in 1995, I didn't know that McNamara had written his memoir about Vietnam. Just before its publication, I received a call from a staff member for ABC-TV's *Prime Time
Live*, informing me that McNamara was going to be inter-
viewed about the book. As part of a selected group of persons
who had been involved directly or indirectly with the war,
Emily and I were each invited to pose a question on air to
McNamara.

The invitation took us by surprise. We were given twenty-four
hours to decide if we would participate. By nature a private person, I instinctively resist the public spotlight, and the request
stirred up painful memories, so I was inclined to decline. But
before I made up my mind, I decided to do a quick read of parts
of *In Retrospect*.

I was moved by McNamara's account of Norman's action. I
was grateful that he had found the honesty and courage to pub-
licly reassess the war and admit that U.S. policy, for which he

bore a heavy responsibility, had been "terribly wrong" and a tragic mistake. It was—and is—extremely rare among public officials to admit error, especially an error of such catastrophic proportions. His final chapter, "Lessons of Vietnam," seemed to me both visionary and practical, setting forth guidelines for the pursuit of international peace.

Emily and I decided to participate in the television program. For me, the decision was made out of respect both for McNamara's courage and for the sacrifice Norman had made. Within hours an ABC crew was at our home, turning our living room into a television studio. Emily had prepared a question concerning help for survivors of the war, and mine dealt with the moral legitimacy of waging war on civilians. In the end, our segment was cut from the program. But other media soon began calling. I decided that a statement from me might be useful. Released through the kind offices of Stony Run Meeting in Baltimore, it said in part:

> *Thirty years ago, on November 2, 1965, Norman Morrison gave his life in agony over our war in Vietnam and in a desperate hope of somehow ending it. . . . To heal the wounds of that war, we must forgive ourselves and each other, and help the people of Vietnam to rebuild their country. I am grateful to Robert McNamara for his courageous and honest reappraisal of the Vietnam war and his involvement in it. I hope this book will contribute to the healing process.*

I enclosed a copy in a personal letter to McNamara. It apparently moved him, perhaps in part because most initial press and public reactions to *In Retrospect* were negative to venomous. A few days later, he called me to thank me for my letter and statement. He told me he was gratified and surprised at the "depth and breadth" of forgiveness I had expressed, then added that he "should have known a Quaker would be that way."

McNamara said that the nation would benefit from my state-ment and asked permission to quote from it, which I gave him. He subsequently referred to it in several public interviews and appearances, and an excerpt appeared at the top of a full-page ad for *In Retrospect* in the *New York Times*. He told me that while he had anticipated that his book would stir things up, he had not reckoned on the full heat of the reaction it received.

Robert McNamara and I had a surprisingly relaxed and can-did conversation. It was almost as if we knew each other, almost as if we hadn't been on opposite sides of the chasm that had split our country apart three decades earlier. Norman's death is a wound that we've both carried. In an odd way, we came into a kind of communion with each other.

We spoke of our emotions, then and now. I told him that the recent past had been very difficult for me, that it seemed I was experiencing Norman's death and loss more emotionally than I had in 1965. He said that, at the time, he could not discuss Norman's self-immolation with his family, even though they were all deeply affected by it. We both confessed that we should have shared more of our feelings with our families.

I told McNamara that Norman had been afraid that Amer-ica might become desperate enough to use nuclear weapons against North Vietnam; that China and the Soviet Union might have moved to defend North Vietnam and the conflict would have escalated into World War III and nuclear holocaust. McNamara responded that Norman was "absolutely right." Using nuclear weapons against North Vietnam was indeed an option that the Joint Chiefs of Staff had presented to President Johnson and McNamara, who had opposed the suggestion. Thankfully, Johnson went along with his Defense Secretary's point of view.

McNamara told me that he shared my belief that we in the United States need to heal the wounds of the Vietnam War and move forward. He said his main concern now is to promote nuclear disarmament and alternatives to war. He is not a paci-fist, but he seemed earnest and sound in his pursuit of peace. I told him that my hope was that reopening our personal and national wounds caused by the war, painful as they were and still are, would be a cleansing process; that it would contribute to a reexamination of our national policies and policymaking. And that, ultimately, maybe we can be healed from that terrible war.

In the spring of 1996, James Carroll's memoir, *An American Requiem: God, My Father, and the War That Came between Us*, won the National Book Awards' first prize for nonfiction. Carroll's father was a high-ranking official in the Pentagon at the time of Norman's death. Carroll wrote that Norman's sacrifice had been a catalyst in his own developing opposition to the war. His tribute to Norman, like the others before it, was heartwarming. But as the twentieth century was drawing to a close, I knew that Norman's witness had become a distant and faded memory for most Americans.

In the spring of 1997, I went to Pendle Hill on a two-week writing retreat. While there, I was invited to share one Sunday afternoon about Norman and this book, which I was just beginning to put on paper. During my presentation, I noticed a young Vietnamese man, Dat Dutinth, whose wife worked at Pendle Hill, standing and holding their beautiful baby boy in his arms. The father and child kept on the edge of the gathering.

When my presentation was over, Dat approached me. He told me that he had been in Saigon when Norman died. His older brothers served in the South Vietnamese Army, and he had barely escaped the draft before emigrating in 1969. Several of his friends had died in the war.

Dat moved to the large table where I had spread some of Norman's writings, along with books, newspaper clippings, letters, and poems about him. The young Vietnamese man immediately picked up the copy of "Emily, My Child." The poem had been written on November 7, 1965, just five days after Norman's sacrifice, by To Huu, North Vietnam's revolutionary poet laureate. Translated by Tran Van Chuong and Felix Greene, it embraces the sharp contrasts of anguished pleas, harsh political indictments, and soft personal touches:

Emily, My Child
Dedicated to Norman R. Morrison

Emily, come with me,
So when grown up you will know the way
and not be lost.
"Where are we going, Daddy?"
"To the riverbank, the Potomac."
"What do you want me to see, Daddy?"
"I want you, dear, to see the Pentagon."
O my child, with your round eyes,
O my child, with your golden hair,
Ask me no more questions, darling!
Come, I will carry you.
Soon you will be home again with Mommy.

Washington,
Twilight . . .
O souls
Living still or having gone before.
Blaze up, Truth, blaze up!
Johnson!
Your crimes are piling high.
All humanity is outraged.
You, the great dollar devil of our world.
You cannot borrow the mantle
Of Christ, nor the saffron robe of Buddha!

McNamara!
Where are you hiding? In the graveyard
Of your vast five-cornered house,
Each corner a continent.
You hide yourself
From the flaming world
As an ostrich hides its head in the burning sand.

Look this way!
For this one moment, look at me!
Here you see not just a man with a child in
his arms.
I am of Today,
And this, my child, my Emily, is the life of all
our Futures.
Here I stand,
And together with me
The great heart of America,
A light to the horizon
A beacon
Of justice.

You gang of devils!
In whose name
Do you send B-52s,
Napalm, and poison gases
From the White House,
From Guam Island,
To Vietnam?
To murder peace and national freedom,
To burn down hospitals and schools,
To kill people who know nothing but love,
To kill children who know nothing but going
to school,
To kill with poisons fields covered with
flowers
and leaves all the four seasons,
To kill even the flow of poetry, song, music
and painting!

In whose name
Do you bury our American youth in coffins?
Young men, strong and handsome,

Able today to release the power of nature
To bring happiness to men!
In whose name
Do you send us to thick jungles
Full of spike pits, of resistance swamps?
To villages and towns which become elusive
fortresses,
Where day and night the earth quakes and the
sky rocks?
O Vietnam, strange land
Where little boys are heroes,
Where hornets are trained as fighters,
Where even flowers and fruit become
weapons!

To hell, to hell with you,
You gang of devils!
And listen, O my America,
To this anguished voice, the never-dying voice
Of this son of yours, a man of this century.

Emily, my darling,
The night is falling. . . .
Tonight I cannot take you home!
After the flames have flared
Mommy will come and fetch you.
Will you hug her and kiss her
For me?
And tell her,
"Daddy's gone gladly, don't be sad."

Washington . . .
Twilight.
O souls
Still living or having gone before!
Now my heart is at its brightest!

> *I burn my body*
> *So the flames may blaze*
> *The Truth.*

"I once knew this poem," Dat whispered to me. "Everyone did." He said that in Vietnam, before Norman's self-immolation, "All we knew about America was bombers and bombs and helicopters and soldiers. Then came Norman Morrison, this voice of conscience." Dat's voice broke and his dark eyes grew moist.

It was a powerful and healing moment for us both. Our exchange unlocked a missing piece of the mystery for me. The realization dawned, and then slowly settled into my heart, that a piece of my healing could only be found on the other side of the world. I was beginning to feel ready to go in search of it.

6

"The Bright Living Torch of Uncle Morrison"

Sacrificing his life for a just cause,
Norman R. Morrison has had his
noble and fine image engraved in
the hearts of our people.
—PHAN THI QUYEN

The Hanoi airport, modest for a capital city's, came into view amid a landscape of lush, green rice paddies. Peasants stooped to work near the runway, their heads covered in wide, cone-shaped straw hats to shelter them from the blazing sun. As our plane touched down, they glanced up in acknowledgment and then went back to their labor.

It was April 1999. I was traveling to Vietnam with Emily and Christina—as Tina now preferred to be called—and their respective partners, Clark Chapin and Jefferson Ryon. We missed Ben, who surely would have been with us if he were living. We also had an unseen member in our little group: Emily was three months pregnant with her first child.

As we landed, I carried in my heart a fervent prayer for strength and the right words to say on this journey that had been both long resisted and long awaited. In a way, it had been in the works for almost thirty-four years. Soon after Norman's death, I had received a call from Louis Schneider, then an associate executive secretary at the American Friends Service Committee's national headquarters in Philadelphia. He asked to visit me in our home in Baltimore. He said he wanted to bring me a message.

A self-contained and proper man, Lou sat in our living room like a parson calling on a newly widowed member of the parish. I had put on my nice blue dress for the occasion, sensing a certain formality was in order. Lou quietly explained that when Norman died, he was in Paris trying to negotiate a settlement of the war, part of the behind-the-scenes peace efforts of the AFSC. He was in the office of Mai Van Bo, the North Vietnamese ambassador to France, to discuss the war and present some proposals. But what Mai Van Bo most wanted to talk about, according to Lou, was Norman's self-immolation, which brought tears to the ambassador's eyes. He asked Lou to deliver personal condolences to me. Lou's own steel-blue eyes welled up as he related these wishes, as did mine.

That was the first of many poignant messages that would come to me from Vietnam, some delivered in person by intermediaries, most in the form of letters and cards. Just four days after Norman's death, I received a letter from Professor Nguyen Van Hieu of the South Vietnam National Front for Liberation. Echoing the sentiments of many of the letters to come, he wrote of his "great admiration" for Norman's "noble self-sacrifice," which "deeply moved all Vietnamese, from the South to the North."

Most of the letters I received came from ordinary Vietnamese people—mothers, farmers, students. A medical student and his two brothers in Hanoi wrote to me, "At this moment, the picture of the bright living torch of Uncle Morrison is flaring up before our eyes." They had received a copy of my statement to the press and ended their letter, "Uncle Morrison was an outstanding son of the United States, and you, Aunt Morrison, have proved to be an honest woman of the United States whom we greatly admire." For the next three years, at Christmas, I received cards and letters in delicately written Vietnamese script. Even though I couldn't understand them, I felt that I knew what they said, and that their sentiments were genuine and heartfelt.

Many letters, including one from the widow of a man who had attempted to assassinate Defense Secretary Robert McNamara while he was on a visit to South Vietnam, expressed great anger or despair about the war and those executing it. Some described in great detail its atrocities and horrors. I felt strangely divided, reading such letters. My broken heart went out to the Vietnamese people in their unspeakable suffering. I felt outrage that we were the cause of most of that pain. Yet I could not condemn our troops, because I knew that they too were suffering. Nor could I demonize our government officials, who were caught in a trap of pride and arrogance.

Gifts also arrived from Vietnam. An official of the Vietnam Women's Union sent a plaque bearing Norman's face. Handmade posters and original pieces of music came from sympathizers throughout the country. Within three weeks of Norman's death, the North Vietnamese government issued a commemorative stamp in his honor. It portrayed Norman's face on a background of flames, above a group of peace marchers carrying placards. Words on the stamp translated, "Norman Morrison, the ultimate sacrifice as duty and purpose demand." Soon after, a street in Hanoi was named in Norman's honor.

For the Vietnamese people, Norman had metaphorically put on the saffron robe of the Buddhist monk and spoken their language. They saw his sacrifice for peace as a great act of love for them. He became a folk hero of sorts, his name rendered in Vietnamese as Mo Ri Xon. He was honored, along with a few other American peace activists, in the November 18, 1965 edition of the *Vietnam Courier*, an English-language newspaper published in Hanoi. An article next to his photo included these words:

> We knew that from the depth of America, proud of its tradition of freedom and democracy, one day a piercing voice would rise. . . . Anne Morrison, mourn over your husband, but be proud of him; millions of Vietnamese women now take you to heart. Weep for your dad, Ben, Tina and Emily Morrison, but be aware that beyond the Pacific, millions

of Vietnamese children have adopted you as their brother
and sisters. Sleep in peace, NORMAN MORRISON, the
flame of your sacrifice will never die down in our hearts.

In a December 11, 1965, *New York Times* interview conducted by a British journalist, North Vietnamese Prime Minister
Pham Van Dong stated that Norman's sacrifice "was so electri-
fying to the Vietnamese that even now, weeks after his death,
they are having public demonstrations in his honor." The interview
was illustrated with a photograph of a North Vietnamese demonstration, in the foreground of which was a young woman wearing a sash bearing Norman's name. "Norman Morrison," continued the prime minister, "has gone into Vietnamese mythology."

That same day, barely a month after Norman's death, I received my first official invitation to visit Vietnam. To my stunned
surprise, Felix Greene, the American writer in London, called to
relay condolences and concern for my family from North Vietnamese President Ho Chi Minh and to extend an invitation from
him for me to visit his country.

I knew that I couldn't make such a trip at that time. The war
was still raging, and my children were my sole responsibility. For
their sakes, I wouldn't knowingly put myself in danger. And I
was concerned that such a visit would appear politically parti-
san and be open to misinterpretation. Although I completely
supported Vietnam's right to self-determination, I was opposed
to the violence of both sides in the conflict.

However, in light of the outpouring of friendship and concern
from the Vietnamese people, I wanted to respond in a manner
that was respectful, positive, and open. I took a train to Philadelphia to consult with Louis Schneider and others at the AFSC
office. We collaborated on this response, which I sent in a night
cable to Greene in London, requesting that he pass it on to Ho
Chi Minh:

*Regarding the two matters you relayed to me on Decem-
ber 11th, may I express my gratitude for the concern shown*

for the material well-being of my family. However, provision for needs has been made and is not a problem.

The matter of a visit is under careful consideration. I am deeply appreciative of the honor of the invitation. My concern is how to search for that response to the invitation which will assuredly further the cessation of the present hostilities and aid in promoting understanding between all parties to the conflict and eventually peace.

Please relay the verbatim contents of this message and regard it all in strict confidence.

Early in the new year, I received, through Greene, a beautiful, lacquered photograph album from Ho Chi Minh, intended as a Christmas gift, which I gratefully acknowledged with a letter "in the spirit of world friendship . . . and the fervent hope that our countries will soon be at peace." I later received from the president an equally lovely lacquered vanity box with mirror, comb, and brush. It held an imprinted card on which was written, in his shaky, elderly script, "Best greetings to Sister Anne & kisses to her dear children."

At that time, no American journalist had been granted permission to travel and report on the war situation in North Vietnam. The *New York Times* was anxious to send a reporter, and Assistant Managing Editor Harrison Salisbury, a Pulitzer Prize-winning journalist, wanted the assignment. Salisbury applied to Hanoi for a visa and waited for several months. When spring arrived and no visa was forthcoming, he contacted me.

I had no idea if I could help Salisbury accomplish his mission, but I respected the integrity of his writing and was more than willing to do what I could to support it. I wrote him a letter on April 12, 1966, which said in part:

At this critical time in international affairs, there is great need here for accurate information about conditions in Vietnam. As a Quaker pacifist, it is my belief that truth itself contains power to evoke change. Presenting Americans with a clearer and truer explanation of the Vietnam trag-edy should increase the possibilities for a peaceful settle-ment.

Current civil strife in South Vietnam points up our sad lack of knowledge of the political situation and the people there. We Americans have an equally acute need to sensi-tively understand the attitudes and aspirations of the North Vietnamese people, to know what they are experiencing in this war conducted in their territory. . . . I believe these needs can be met by first-hand reporting from within North and South Vietnam by newsmen such as you who have a reputation for objectivity and honesty.

Eight days later, I received a gracious letter from Salisbury, thanking me for my help. He eventually received his visa, mak-ing him the first American reporter allowed into North Vietnam during the war and marking a breakthrough in reportage on the war in the United States. When he came to Greensboro College as a guest lecturer a few years later, I was invited to accompany him and his wife to a dinner in his honor. It was a pleasure to be with this gracious couple and finally to meet the journalist with whom fate had connected me during the war.

In his 1967 book, *Behind the Lines—Hanoi*, Salisbury ac-knowledged my support in getting his visa and wrote about Norman's significance in Vietnam:

I sent new letters and cablegrams, more in stubbornness than in expectation, reminding Hanoi of my deep and con-tinuing interest. No reply was forthcoming. Then . . . I won a fine and unexpected supporter for my project—Anne Morrison, widow of Norman Morrison, the American Quaker who had burned himself to death before the Pen-tagon, sacrificing his life in an effort to arouse the con-science of America against the war in Vietnam.

Morrison had become a saint in North Vietnam—much more than a hero. His name was reverenced and, I was told, every North Vietnamese child knew his story. Mrs. Morrison wrote a letter in my behalf. I do not know precisely how to evaluate its effects. But after I reached Hanoi and learned of the sanctity in which Morrison's memory was held, I came to feel that Mrs. Morrison's letter, simple and direct, had probably been my best credential in getting the visa. Not only was Morrison a shining light in North Vietnam, but his widow and child were equally venerated throughout the land.

Much later, we would learn in Vietnam that nothing had imprinted Norman's sacrifice in the conscience and memory of the Vietnamese people as To Huu's poem, "Emily, My Child."

Harrison Salisbury's request for help was just one of several that came to me in the spring of 1966. As the war intensified and the suffering escalated, many people on both sides of the world were seeking new ideas and ways to resolve the conflict. Mme. Bui Thi Cam, deputy to Vietnam's National Assembly, sent to me on behalf of the Vietnamese Mothers Group "A Letter to American Mothers," pleading for help in persuading the Johnson administration to end U.S. involvement in Vietnam.

From around the United States, as word spread of the high esteem in which the Vietnamese people held Norman, individuals and groups sent letters requesting my help in establishing contact with North Vietnam. Some came from families desperately trying to locate their loved ones in the military who were missing in action or being held as prisoners of war. I was more than eager to send letters of inquiry to Ho Chi Minh on their behalf.

Other requests came from groups desiring to launch friendship visits and humanitarian service projects. The American Friends Service Committee, with its clear commitment to addressing suffering on all sides of a conflict, desired to expand its efforts beyond its daycare center and prosthesis-and-rehabilitation clinic in South Vietnam's Quang Ngai province to include such services in the North. I tried to respond to this and every request for help in a positive way, believing that using the access

I was granted was one more way to ensure that Norman had not sacrificed himself in vain.

When I wrote a letter of support for a group of American women desiring to make a peace visit to North Vietnam, I received a response from an official of the Vietnam Women's Union. She hoped that my children were "delighted with the small gifts of their Vietnamese aunts" that had been sent to them. And she wrote, after seeing their picture, "We long for an opportunity to hug our beloved Ben, Tina, and Emily and tell them that thousands and thousands of Vietnamese aunts are fond of them. I am very moved to see you and your children in the photo, especially as Ben is the very image of his father."

Anxious to do whatever I could to try to end the war, I consulted that spring with Fr. Philip Berrigan—who lived in Baltimore and, along with his brother, Fr. Daniel Berrigan, was on the front lines of Catholic resistance to the war—about involving Pope Paul VI. He didn't think this idea as wild as I thought he might. Philip Berrigan, Harry Niles, and I met with Baltimore's Lawrence Cardinal Sheehan to discuss sending a letter asking for the pope's intervention, which the cardinal agreed to relay.

My letter to Pope Paul VI said, in part: "Your great concern for world peace has inspired many of us to search more creatively for a solution to the war in Vietnam. I ask you to consider inviting to the Vatican high-ranking emissaries of the governments of the United States, South Vietnam, North Vietnam, and the National Liberation Front." I offered to write to Ho Chi Minh to encourage his participation.

These many years later, I am still amazed that I found the audacity to draft a letter to the Vatican, but, in that time of crisis, we were willing to do audacious things. I have no idea if my letter had any effect. But I was pleased to read some time later that Pope Paul VI had, according to a June 29, 1968, *Washington Post* article, "initiated secret, months-long contacts with North Vietnam to try to arrange Vietnam peace talks."

In the summer of 1967, I wrote to Ho Chi Minh on behalf of A Quaker Action Group, a new U.S. peace organization that wanted to sail a boat filled with medical supplies from Japan into North Vietnam's Haiphong Harbor. Concerned for the safety of the Quakers, the North Vietnamese president replied that it was "not convenient" for the boat and its volunteers to go to North Vietnam, as the United States was "intensifying its barbarous air raids" on the country. But the undaunted Quakers went anyway.

Thirty-four years passed before I mustered the emotional courage to go to Vietnam. Other invitations had come, one connected with the dedication of the Vietnamese-American Peace Park near Hanoi in 1995, and another requesting me as a sponsor of a reconciliation bike trip from Hanoi to Ho Chi Minh City (formerly Saigon) involving veterans from both sides of the war. What finally prompted me was a letter that I received in March 1998, postmarked Hanoi, from the U.S. Embassy. After being repeatedly prodded by Bob Hull, a former college classmate of Norman's, Pete Peterson, the U.S. ambassador to Vietnam, sent me a warm note of encouragement to visit.

I will never forget receiving the ambassador's letter. My hands shook as I opened it. It was like a key turning in a lock. Perhaps official words from my own country were what I had been waiting for, for years, without even realizing it. While I had received sympathetic sentiments from government officials in both North and South Vietnam after Norman's death, my own government had been silent. I didn't realize how much that silence hurt until I received Peterson's letter.

So . . . it was time. Not knowing what I would find in Vietnam, or what would be asked of my family and me, I simply gave myself to the journey. What I most wanted was to be able to thank personally the Vietnamese people for their sympathy and kindness after Norman's death. I also hoped that I could finally move beyond my wounds by facing them on this trip, in that place. Meeting the Vietnamese people would surely bring me face to face with my past. I thought I was healed enough to face Vietnam—maybe just enough.

Before we flew halfway around the world to this land so different from ours, a friend gave me a note bearing a quotation from the impressionist painter Renoir, who said that to be an artist is to be "a cork carried on the water." I saw myself as that flimsy, insubstantial cork. I felt vulnerable, traveling to a "Great Unknown." I recognized some of my fears as irrational—that we would drown in a plane crash over the ocean, or contract malaria, or step on one of the countless land mines left from the war, still buried in the soil of Vietnam and still wounding and killing innocent people. A far more realistic fear was that I would experience an emotional upheaval I couldn't handle; that I would be done in by an avalanche of grief.

From time to time I wondered where my daughters and I found the emotional energy to go. We seemed so distant from the war then—more than three decades removed in time. But the truth is that the war was still inside us. I knew that this trip was a critical step on my journey to wholeness. My mantra was a quotation from Julia Cameron's *Blessings*: "Within me, I carry God. Within God, I am carried." The mysterious paradox of being held by God, and at the same time carrying that of God within me, rang true to my spiritual experience and belief. That was my comfort.

I was also reassured by the knowledge that many people were symbolically accompanying us on this journey of friendship and reconciliation with our traumatic past. Fellow Quakers, friends, and strangers had helped us through their financial support and promises of prayers. One friend had told me that she would light a candle for us every day we were in Vietnam. Others had said that this was healing for them, that this was their journey, too. I didn't understand how a healing process for me could also work for others, but that became much clearer after we returned and I shared the stories of our trip.

Early one morning at home, just before I left, I wrote a statement to the people of Vietnam to carry with me and distribute. It said in part:

> *Norman and I . . . considered all the people of the world to be one family. Thus, you are our brothers and sisters,*

and we are your family. We were his family whom he
loved, yet he considered the people of Vietnam to be his
family as well.

Norman's sacrifice transcended the boundaries of na-
tionality and politics and war. He paid the ultimate price
for his passionate beliefs with his life. Our family paid a
lasting price, too, because of his loss. . . .

Some of our veterans are still wounded in heart and
mind by the war. I hope many more of them will come to
Vietnam, as we have, and be healed. If they could see how
the Vietnamese people have bound up their wounds,
grieved their losses, rebuilt their lives and country, and
moved beyond enmity and sorrow, they would surely be
encouraged and blessed.

We are encouraged and blessed by the friendship and
love of the Vietnamese people and their powerful spirit of
hope, all of which is healing for us. We thank them for
these gifts. We are honored to be in Vietnam.

On the flight to Los Angeles, the man sitting next to me asked
where I was going. I felt guarded, and all I could answer was,
"On a sentimental journey to Vietnam." He seemed surprised.
Our conversation ended with that brief exchange.

At a moment during the fifteen-hour flight from Los Angeles
to Hong Kong, I waited outside a cabin lavatory next to a bald,
energetic American. He remarked, "It used to take us twenty-one
days to make this journey." I knew before asking him that he was
also headed to Vietnam.

In the Hong Kong airport, he joined a group of about twenty
men, wearing special name tags on their jackets, evidently all ex-
GIs—war buddies returning together to the place that had forged
their bond through trial and trauma. I encountered him again in
a line in the terminal, and he asked me where I was headed. This
time, I felt ready to talk. I explained to him as simply as I could.
His mouth fell open in astonishment. "I'm sorry," he said.

"That's OK," I replied calmly, holding in my emotion. "It's all right." I wanted to believe that it was.

The man abruptly left the line and rejoined his group a little distance away, apparently retelling my story, gesturing with great feeling. From time to time I thought of those ex-soldiers while we were in Vietnam, wondering if they were revisiting places that wouldn't leave them or mourning fallen comrades. I was glad in my heart that they were returning, that they had the opportunity to see this country at peace. My prayer for them echoed my own—that whatever wounds they were still carrying would be healed in Vietnam.

After a grueling twenty-four hours in transit, we arrived in Hanoi exhausted, yet full of excitement and anticipation. Hoang Cong Thuy, secretary general of the Vietnam-U.S. Friendship Society (VUS), greeted us at the airport with his wonderfully open smile and bouquets of roses—the first of many flowers we would receive as we traveled throughout Vietnam. Thuy's daughter was a student at George School near Philadelphia, a Quaker school that Emily had also attended. We shared with him the Quaker saying "I will hold you in the Light." It fascinated him, and during the week that he served as our guide, he found several occasions to practice his newfound expression.

Scarcely any time elapsed before Thuy and two young clerks at the airport shyly approached Emily, nodding and tugging at her sleeve, each declaring, "I know the poem 'Emily.'" We were told that adults in both the North and the South—and every schoolchild in the North—had memorized To Huu's long, passionate poem. Schools in Vietnam taught it as late as 1980, and it has entered the literary history of the country.

Because Emily had been in her father's arms before he died at the Pentagon and had lived, she became a symbol of hope and survival for the Vietnamese during the war, at a time when their own children were being wounded and killed, their families and homes were being shattered, and the very future of their country was uncertain. Because of the poem, Emily, it seemed, had become a kind of icon in Vietnam.

Waiting outside for us in a van was our other guide, Ha Van An, an editor with the Vietnam Journalists Association. Also present were Lady Borton and Phoung, the seasoned and resourceful leaders of Quaker Service, the AFSC office in Hanoi. For weeks and months before we left America, they had diligently worked with representatives of VUS to arrange a full agenda for our visit. Dave Elder of the AFSC in Philadelphia and Mike Boehm, an ex-GI from Madison, Wisconsin, who was deeply involved with peace projects and community development in Vietnam, accompanied us on the drive through Hanoi's narrow streets. Each of these friends would be at our side in invaluable ways as we experienced Vietnam.

We arrived at the simple Quaker Service headquarters in the courtyard of the old La Thanh Hotel, where we were to stay for the week. Relaxing around a round table in the lobby, we were treated to the first of many delicious meals in Vietnam: a small bowl of rice for each of us and communal bowls of green beans, pork, tomatoes with dumplings, sauteed vegetables, and shrimp.

Bone-tired that night, I felt we could have slept for the next twenty-four hours. We had been immensely relieved to hear that the next day's schedule would be light. Light, indeed. At precisely eight o'clock the following morning, we found ourselves being marched two by two down the broad Boulevard Duong Hung Vuong in front of the Ho Chi Minh Mausoleum and Museum. Our escorts were two young men in bright red-and-white military uniforms. Even at that early hour, a long line of Vietnamese citizens was slowly moving on the sidewalk in front of the mausoleum, waiting to see the impeccably preserved body of Ho Chi Minh—Uncle Ho to his people—lying in state. At the entrance, the uniformed men each picked up a standing wreath of flowers and placed it on either side of the main door, on our behalf.

Our visit to the museum was too brief to do justice to the impressive artifacts of the life and times of Ho Chi Minh, along with historical displays of concurrent world developments. Even so, we got some sense of the amazing life of Ho—militant anti-colonial nationalist, scholar, revolutionary—who became convinced that Communism was the key to the emancipation of oppressed people in Vietnam, if not the world. Ho Chi Minh was also a poet. A friend gave me one of his poems, written while he was in prison, after I returned home. It speaks of the sensitivities we encountered on our trip:

> *Although they have tightly bound*
> *my arms and legs,*
> *All over the mountain I hear the song of birds,*
> *And the forest is filled*
> *with the perfume of spring flowers.*
> *Who can prevent me from freely enjoying these,*
> *Which take from the long journey*
> *a little of its loneliness?*

At the museum, we were abruptly ushered into a small reception room for a surprise visit with Vu Ky, former President Ho Chi Minh's personal secretary. Vu Ky was an elderly man full of jokes, reminiscences, and personal history. Seated around a long, low table, we were served cups of strong French coffee and Vietnamese green tea, mango halves, and a colorfully fascinating tropical fruit called dragon's teeth.

Vu Ky insisted that Emily sit next to him, in the obvious seat of honor. Alone among our family, only Emily, at the unspeakably tender age of one, had witnessed her father's horrifying death. Still, we were unprepared to deal with the consistent level of attention showered on her. Being pregnant and so much in the limelight made it doubly hard on Emily.

Unexpectedly, at the end of our first full day in Vietnam, I came face to face with the one thing I most feared about this journey. I was feeling exhausted, but I couldn't sleep. It seemed that my daughters and I were all tumbling together in a wringer of emotions. I felt helpless and overwhelmed with the responsibility for the trip on my shoulders. Questions raced through my mind: How will it go? Will we say the right things (whatever they are)? Will each of us be able to hold up under the pressure? How will it feel to encounter Norman over and over again through the eyes and hearts of the Vietnamese people?

Then . . . it happened. I did what I should have done thirty-four years before. I began to grieve deeply, to moan and keen Norman's passing. I let out all the collected emotions—grief, bitterness, guilt, sadness, and, yes, anger. I wailed and raged at Norman for leaving me at the age of thirty with such challenges, and for abandoning his children. I felt completely alone.

My wailing might have lasted thirty minutes, or an hour, or two hours, I really don't know. I only hoped that no one heard me through the hotel walls. I eventually just cried myself out. Then, finally, I was able to pray: "Lord, help me. I cannot carry this load anymore. I cannot carry this little family by myself." It was all I could do. After I prayed, I fell asleep.

The next morning, I awoke tired but cleansed, with a new sense of peace. My prayer lingered in my heart: "Today, Lord, let me lean on thee. I don't have to, and can't anyway, hold up this family any more. Let me be that cork on your water."

Despite the pain I encountered there, there was no doubt in my mind that going to Vietnam was what I had needed to do. Maybe it was, in the end, a matter of faith. It felt right and also timely for Christina, Emily, and me to do this together. During our visit, several Vietnamese asked, "Why did you wait so long?" My answer was always the same: "We could not have come a day earlier." Even then, after thirty-four years, we were scarcely prepared.

Two days after our arrival, on a bright and warm Sunday, we drove north to Bac Giang province, about thirty kilometers from Hanoi. We wanted to hold a memorial service for Norman at the Peace Park there. Sponsored by veterans in both the United States and Vietnam, the park is a project of the Madison, Wisconsin, Friends Meeting. Trees have been planted there to honor those who died on both sides of the war.

On the way to the park, we stopped at the provincial government headquarters for a formal greeting ceremony, and also at a village school. The schoolchildren, with happy, beautifully expressive faces and shiny, black hair—all dressed in white shirts and dark trousers or skirts—were waiting for us in the schoolyard. They presented us with bouquets of fresh, hand-picked flowers. It was a beautiful, shining moment in the Sunday sun.

Afterward, we crowded into a simple schoolroom filled with small desks and heard the principal of the school give an enthusiastic speech of welcome. As I responded, I couldn't help thinking of Ben, who would have enjoyed so much being with us there. I felt his spirit present.

The Peace Park, located on a small hill overlooking a valley green with rice paddies, is a place of beauty and serenity. There, with a group of mostly veteran-aged Vietnamese men and women and three of the young schoolgirls, we planted a large banyan tree with spreading roots in Norman's memory. Farther down on a small slope, Christina and Emily each planted a longan fruit tree, an evergreen native to Southeast Asia, for their dad.

A small, oilcloth-covered table decorated with flowers and incense sticks had been set up on the hill. We each in turn burned incense and bowed silently in memory of Norman. I placed a photograph of him and a commemorative plaque on the table. Through the kindness of Mike Boehm, a Vietnamese craftsman had made the plaque, which would be affixed to the banyan tree. It reads:

Norman R. Morrison, Dec. 29, 1933 – Nov. 2, 1965.
American Quaker, World Citizen.
One life given for one world, one human family.

Shoveling dirt around the roots of the banyan tree that day while brushing away my tears, I realized—incredibly, for the first time—how important it was to plant something green and alive in Norman's memory. The tree-planting ceremony symbolically embedded Norman in the soil of Vietnam, though I recognized at that moment that he was already there. Norman belongs to the people of Vietnam and to their history as surely as he belongs to us and ours.

While Christina and Emily were planting their trees, Nguyen Ngoc Hung—who with Mike was the original inspiration behind the Vietnamese-American Peace Parks—quietly approached us. A professor of linguistics at the Hanoi University of Foreign Studies, Hung is highly articulate, gentle, and sincere. Tears welled up in his large, brown eyes as he recalled hearing of Norman's self-immolation.

"I was a member of the National Liberation Front during the American War," he explained. "I guess you would have called me a Viet Cong." Hung looked like anything but the stereotypical Viet Cong soldier, who had been portrayed in the United States as an unfeeling, ruthless fighter for Communism. "Heading south along the Ho Chi Minh trail," said Hung, "I was in my bunker in the jungle that night when the news of Morrison's death came over Liberation Radio. I just sat there and cried. That someone in America cared enough about us that he would give up his life . . . "

Hung's voice broke before he could finish. That was my first realization that what moved Hung and others so profoundly was that someone in America would die for them.

Norman had given his life for people who had been conquered, ruled, and dominated by one colonial power after another for more than a thousand years. First China, then France and Japan, and finally the United States, had tried to determine and control their future.

Norman had embraced the people and traditions of Vietnam with his death, wrapping himself in the Buddhist garment of flames and becoming, in their words, "a torch of liberty." This earned him, according to the Vietnamese, "a place in our hearts forever." We heard those words over and over all across Vietnam. At virtually every stop, what people most wanted to do in our presence was tell the stories of where they had been when they heard the news of Norman's sacrifice—often with tears streaming down their faces.

Hung was the first to tell us his story, and I was moved by his emotion and his generous spirit. A week later, the evening before we left Hanoi for our time in the South of Vietnam, Hung came by the Quaker Service office to say goodbye. In his hand was a decorative container of Vietnamese tea, a gift for us. Tears welled up again in his dark eyes when he said: "Thank you for coming to Vietnam. Your visit is a gift from God."

After the memorial service for Norman, we visited a Buddhist pagoda in a nearby village. It was tended by a friendly, vivacious group of village women, many of them elderly, diminutive, and dressed in brown robes and hats. Lined up along the steps of the pagoda, they had been anxiously awaiting our arrival. Around them and out into the bare courtyard were villagers of all ages, murmuring excitedly.

It was very warm, even stuffy, inside the pagoda as we took turns burning incense at the altar, elaborately decorated and filled with various representations of the Buddha, floral arrangements, fruit, and rice balls wrapped in brightly colored cellophane. The atmosphere was also warm with emotion. Two of the women stood up together and, with an enchanting mix of embarrass-ment and enthusiasm, sang a song of welcome they had written in our honor. We applauded, and then the crowd erupted in an affectionate frenzy of hugs and greetings. We felt kin to those women; they seemed more like aunts and grandmothers than strangers.

Later, at a spirited luncheon back at the Bac Giang provincial headquarters, Christina's partner, Jefferson, was "adopted" by the men at our table, who no doubt had downed too many vodka toasts. They were so impressed with the way he had handled a shovel at the Peace Park that they invited him to come back to Vietnam and help them with their orchards. I wondered if Jefferson would want to do that very thing.

Although traveling primarily to support Christina, Jefferson was on his own personal journey of healing. When he was a young boy, the Vietnam War had taken his father, too. A career Air Force officer and aerial photographer, his Dad had crashed while taking off just across the border in Thailand on a mission. Jefferson harbored a hope to someday find the spot where his father had died.

I wondered if any of us would ever return. Would Christina and Emily ever go back to the Peace Park to visit the trees they had planted in honor of their father, maybe bringing along our grandchildren? Would I ever come back to this place?

Christina was only five years old at the time of the first memorial service for her father and doesn't remember much of that day. Emily had been too young to attend. On that hill and in the pagoda in Bac Giang, both of them, then in their thirties, were able to honor their father in a way they hadn't before. The experience inspired Christina to write a poem:

Peace Pagoda

High on a hill
the peace dove settles at last.
Let us walk together
young and old,
children leading the way
through soft green rice
paddies
up the gentle slope
to the pagoda.

Now is the time
this is the place
we have all awaited.
No solemn sermons
from long benches,
just the smiles of children
bringing flowers in the sun.
Let us burn incense
and offer prayers—
a spirit lasts forever
on the wind.

> *Water the tree*
> *we plant together*
> *with your tears.*
> *It will live 1,000 years*
> *and bear delicious fruit.*
> *Plant two more*
> *for all the children*
> *without fathers,*
> *standing tall,*
> *reaching their branches*
> *toward the sky.*
>
> *Buddha songs drift*
> *across the paddies.*
> *Once my country rained fire*
> *on your people.*
> *Now we walk down the hill*
> *together, laughing,*
> *to the temple of our friends.*

I wouldn't take anything for the joy I felt, and still feel, upon reading Christina's tender and beautiful poem, and the healing of a deep wound toward which it points. I hope and trust that the memories of that day will help us finally to accept our loss, knowing that, as Christina said, "a spirit lasts forever on the wind." And in many, many hearts.

7

An Arrow of Love

The Vietnamese people, when
fighting oppression, always had in
their heart the image
of Norman Morrison.
—FORMER NORTH VIETNAMESE PRIME
MINISTER PHAM VAN DONG

$\mathcal{H}$anoi—ancient, crowded, and fascinating—was the base for
our busy week of travels in the North. For the most part, our
precious bits of free time were very early in the day, or late in the
evening. I enjoyed early morning solo walks down Pho Doi Can
Street from our hotel to buy freshly baked French rolls for our
breakfast at the Quaker Service office. It was wonderful to maneu-
ver Hanoi sidewalks in anonymity, stepping around entrepreneurs
busily hawking everything from tropical fruit and postcards to
bike repairs and noodle soup. Most people smiled at me. A few
seemed to want to practice their English, saying "Hello!" and following their enthusiastic greeting with, "Are you an American?"

As we traveled around the countryside, we saw a poor nation
still struggling to reconstruct after our devastating war. At every
"official" stop we made, I was expected to rise and respond to
speeches of welcome. I guess I developed a rather standard response, because my daughters began to kid me. "Mother, just let
the translators do your speech," they teased. "Thuy and An already know what you are going to say!"

"OK, you give the speech next time," I rejoined. And so
Christina and Emily began to speak up more often.

We visited the beautiful Presidential Palace, which French governors had occupied during the colonial era. As president, Ho Chi Minh had chosen not to live there, but rather to reside in a simple, open house on stilts he had built nearby for both his personal and official use. Mme. Nguyen Thi Binh, vice president of the government of Vietnam, officially welcomed our family to the palace.

Mme. Truong My Hoa, vice president of the National Assembly, then greeted us in a large, formal reception suite. While reflecting great dignity and reserve, she was visibly moved when she offered us her country's "condolences in person." She explained that during the war she had been a political prisoner in the South. She spent several years in the infamous "tiger cages" of Con Son Island, a notorious torture center in the South China Sea. The concrete cages were nine-by-five-foot structures, barred across the top, open to rain and sun and the lime that patrolling guards threw on the prisoners crowded below.

My Hoa said that when she and the other prisoners heard the news of Norman's sacrifice, they made an altar and held a memorial service for him in prison. Tears welled up in her eyes as she recounted her memories, and tears were in the eyes of many of us in that room as well. She had suffered much in prison, she said, and she and her fellow prisoners had drawn strength from Norman's suffering. "If we grew discouraged, we would remember Morrison. He had sacrificed himself because he cared about our people. Surely we women in prison could muster the courage to survive, continue the struggle, and rebuild the peace."

I looked around that fine room, with its lovely woodwork and brocade-covered chairs, so distant from the horror of the tiger cages. My Hoa had said when we entered, "This is where we meet our highest-level official visitors." Turning to me, she had added, "And this is where we meet our closest friends."

After meeting these two distinguished women, I was full of anticipation about our conversation with U.S. Ambassador Pete Peterson. It seemed ironic and sad, however, that our only encounter in Vietnam with armed guards, metal detectors, and camera restrictions was at our own U.S. Embassy. However, once we passed through those barriers, we found the staff and the ambassador friendly and welcoming. Informal in shirtsleeves, Peterson invited us into his large office, where we talked with him for an hour. The discussion focused on economics and the hopeful future of less restrictive trade between the United States and Vietnam. The ambassador didn't refer to our personal history or inquire about our visit, seeming not to want to dwell on our awkward, painful past.

Of all our meetings in Vietnam, our time with former Prime Minister Pham Van Dong was a special treasure. He, along with Ho Chi Minh and Gen. Vo Nguyen Giap, had governed the country during the war, until Ho's death in 1969. During that time period, I had an indirect personal connection with Pham Van Dong.

In 1968, the American Friends Service Committee was trying to extend to North Vietnam the same prosthetic-and-rehabilitation services to wounded Vietnamese that they were operating in the South. That summer, Stewart Meacham, the AFSC national peace secretary, traveled to Hanoi to meet with Pham Van Dong about this humanitarian effort. The prime minister sent his personal condolences to me through Stewart and also issued another invitation to me to come to Vietnam. It was from that visit by Stewart that I learned that Norman's picture had been prominently displayed in a Hanoi museum, and that a North Vietnamese movie about the efforts of a truck driver to deliver important materials south of the Demilitarized Zone showed a closeup of two photographs hung in the cab of his truck: one was of Ho Chi Minh, the other of Norman.

In his home—a palatial, formal, French Colonial building near Ho Chi Minh's house—Pham Van Dong stood waiting, dressed in a casual white suit. When we arrived, he moved stiffly forward to greet us. Although in his nineties, blind, and wearing a hearing aid, Pham Van Dong was alert and sharp despite the infirmities of advanced age.

"This is a memorable day for me," said the elder statesman, with a warm and fervent spirit. He added, "But it is regretful that

Uncle Ho is not here with us. I believe you know very well how much Ho Chi Minh appreciated the great sacrifice of the peace fire of Norman Morrison." When I asked him what the former president would want between our two countries if he were alive, Pham Van Dong replied that Ho would want us "to replace animosity with mutual friendship, cooperation, and mutual assistance."

The former prime minister wished us "beautiful days" in Vietnam and told us, "Your visit to Vietnam after more than thirty years is very precious to me." I thanked him and told him how much the expressions of admiration and sympathy from the Vietnamese people had meant to me after Norman's death, how deeply moved I was that his people embraced us and affirmed one human family of American and Vietnamese. "Your family is esteemed to the highest magnitude," he said. He responded to comments from Christina and Jefferson about the spiritual integrity of the Vietnamese people by saying, "Let me call you my grandchildren."

I shared with Pham Van Dong something Norman had said to me more than once. "Norman believed that society needs a few people who will go beyond normal expectations," I said, "and that sacrifice is sometimes necessary for a larger cause. My family was wounded by his sacrifice, but we understand."

The former prime minister said of Norman's self-immolation, "That anyone at a moment can do something so beautiful and noble, well, it's unimaginable." He added that Norman's "noble and great act" had touched "the most beautiful and valuable parts in humanity." And he said, "Therefore, I think Norman Morrison with his sacrifice has become immortal."

I told Pham Van Dong that I was impressed by the combination of warrior strength and tenderness in the Vietnamese people. He answered: "Thank you. You speak the truth." He spoke of the Buddhist and Taoist virtues of frugality, truthfulness, and humility, qualities celebrated in Lao-Tzu's *Tao Te Ching*. When I told him that Norman and I had read the *Tao Te Ching* and found it compatible with our Quaker faith in its compassion and simplicity, he exclaimed, "Exactly! I love you."

Over and over during our hour together, Pham Van Dong emphasized that the Vietnamese people of the war period held Norman in their hearts as a shining example of courage and strength. More than once, he referred to Norman as "a noble saint, the highest ideal." When I protested that Norman had feet of clay just like the rest of us, Pham Van Dong smiled, then raised his fist in the air, insisting, "But he was a saint to us!" Bringing his fist down, he beat upon his chest and proclaimed, "And he will live forever in our hearts."

Before we left, I gave Pham Van Dong a handmade scrapbook—twenty or so pages of articles, photographs, poems, and letters about Norman. With the inspiration and great assistance of Lady Borton, we had assembled the scrapbooks after our arrival in Hanoi. They were enthusiastically received at every official visit we made. Whenever we ran out, Lady worked early and late cranking out more booklets on the Quaker Service mimeograph machine.

The front page portrayed a small photograph of Norman. Pham Van Dong was too blind to see the scrapbook, so I described its contents. He thanked me profusely, then leaned down and kissed the front of the book. "You just kissed Norman's picture," I told him. Hardly waiting for the translation, he exclaimed with a smile, "Good!"—and then kissed it again. "This is a friend whom I have never met in actual life," he said, "but I always met in my spiritual life."

When it was time to part, Pham Van Dong took my hands in his and said with great feeling, "This is one of the happiest days of my life." His declaration mirrored my own emotion. Then, in a dignified and courtly fashion, he bent down and kissed my hands. It was an unforgettable moment, especially poignant in my memory, as the elder statesman died a year after our visit. After our meeting, I wrote in my journal, "I am realizing more and more that life requires of us a great courage, combined with tenderness, trust, and faith."

The able young interpreter at our meeting with Pham Van Dong was Biu The Giang, who had studied at Johns Hopkins

University in Baltimore, where we were living at the time of Norman's death. I felt an instant rapport with this delightful man, who was young enough to be my son. Giang came by the Quaker Service office early the next morning, carrying a large, blue velvet box in his arms. It held an exquisitely carved wooden statue of The Compassionate Buddha with a Thousand Hands, a gift from Pham Van Dong. I was overwhelmed at such a beautiful and thoughtful gift.

After our visit with the former prime minister, I thought our meeting later that morning with our co-hosts, the Vietnam-American Society, would be anticlimactic. But that was not at all the case. We were ushered into a modest room and were seated on one side of a long table. The VUS staff sat across from us. After warm greetings, Vu Xuan Hong, the VUS executive vice president, gestured to his colleagues and said to us, "Now, several of us have some personal words to say to you."

One after another, they told us where they were when they heard of Norman's self-immolation. They wanted us to know how it had felt to them personally—indeed, how it had changed their lives. Hong and three of his colleagues were middle-school students at the time. They all had learned the "Emily poem" in school.

Khong Dai Minh stood up to tell his story. "I was a water buffalo boy," said this tall, craggy man with high cheekbones. During the war, he had been a child living in a rural province north of Hanoi, in a poor village where no one had access to a newspaper. "No one except the headmaster of my village school had a radio," Minh explained. "One day, the headmaster called us all together and told us about Morrison. Tears were streaming down his face. Of course, we all cried. I could not believe someone in another country would die for us."

As he was relating his story, the grown-up water buffalo boy wept again, as did all of us in the room. In that moment, I received a clear image. It seemed that Norman's act had shot an arrow of love from America, which traveled halfway around the world and gently pierced the hearts of the Vietnamese people. That such a thing had ever happened was amazing enough. Even more amazing was that this arrow of love was still lodged in their hearts.

Then it was the turn of Pham Khac Lam, who appeared to be the oldest member of the VUS staff. He was a journalist in 1965, charged with writing about the American War and encouraging his fellow citizens to resistance. "But how could we, a small, poor nation, hope to resist and repel a large and strong giant like America?" he asked. "It was like a gnat fighting an elephant." Then suddenly Lam threw his arms up in a wide arc and exclaimed, "Then came the sacrifice of Morrison, a blazing light which lit up the sky, a flame of liberty and hope!"

Over lunch, Hong told me about his mother. "I am an only child. My name, Vu Xuan Hong, means Rain Spring Rose—like the flower. I was like a rose to my mother, who resisted during the French War." While his mother was pregnant with Hong, the French imprisoned her in Saigon. "She was repeatedly beaten," said Hong. "But she always turned her back to protect her unborn child in the womb. When I was old enough, she showed me the scars on her back from the beatings."

Hong turned around, and with his fingers he indicated on his own back where the scars had been on the back of his mother. This successful young diplomat, member of the National Assembly, still symbolically carried his beloved mother's wounds. Yet when Hong told me this story, he showed no evidence of hatred for the French in his voice or his words. He seemed more collected than I, hearing his poignant story.

At the end of that full and emotional day, I took some time before sleep to write again in my journal. I was filled with a sense of being upheld by love, by prayers, and by friends back home. I wrote: "Over and over on this trip, I feel uplifted by God's hand."

Our next excursion was to Thanh Hoa province, once an ancient region of historical importance, now a poor agrarian region bordering the sea, where Quaker Service sponsors a community development project. After a few hours of travel, we arrived in the evening, weary and hot, at the Thanh Hoa Hotel.

How surprised we were to walk into the lobby and find a welcoming party of provincial leaders, dressed up and smiling broadly, awaiting our arrival! Although I was embarrassed at my disheveled appearance, the Vietnamese politely seemed not to notice.

We joined our hosts at a delicious dinner, complete with the now-customary welcoming toasts and speeches. After the meal, there were tears and hugs when Christina and Emily read aloud poems they had written on the trip. How affirmed the girls seemed, and how happy that made me feel. We were discovering a large, extended family in Vietnam.

We weren't the only ones celebrated at the dinner. Toward the end of the evening, the spotlight was turned on a beaming and vivacious woman, who looked to be about fifty-five years old. During the war, this sturdy woman had carried nearly twice her weight in artillery on her back—about one hundred kilos, or 220 pounds—up a nearby mountain to an anti-aircraft group. The anti-aircraft outfit was trying to defend her village and a strategic bridge against the bombs of U.S. B-52s. Because of her courageous action, she had been named a heroine of the war.

Earlier that evening, just outside of Thanh Hoa along Highway 1, I think we crossed that very bridge. I could visualize the woman laboring up the mountain. It gave me an odd and sad feeling to think that the Vietnamese at the bridge were shooting at our aircraft. Of course, they were protecting their village. I tried to imagine what a B-52 would sound like overhead, or a Huey helicopter, and bombs dropping on my village, with all the devastation and suffering. In their shoes, would I have felt compelled to do the same? Would I have felt it necessary to haul artillery up that mountain on my back, and would I have found the strength and courage to do it?

That evening, our family finally had some time to talk among ourselves. We discussed the paradox of Norman's act. We all knew that he was a dedicated pacifist and that he was demanding, with the ultimate power of his life, an end to the war. Norman and I both believed that the United States should call for a cease fire, withdraw from Vietnam, and support a diplomatic settlement according to the Geneva Accords of 1954. The accords, drawn up after the defeat of the French in Vietnam, provided a way for Vietnam to become a unified nation, free of outside interference and domination.

The word from the war heroine and others that Norman's act had moved them to greater efforts in defense of their country troubled me. It was hard to hear that Norman's sacrifice of his life had, among other things, encouraged violence, albeit in the cause of Vietnamese self-determination. I knew Norman did not want another person to die in that war—not another Vietnamese man, woman, or child, and not another American soldier. It was a senseless war that never should have been.

Christina, Jefferson, and I had raised this concern with Vu Xuan Hong and his staff around the table at the VUS meeting. Hong listened attentively, then responded: "Mrs. Anne, we were fighting for our country and our land. We did not want to be dominated by outsiders anymore. We would have fought to the last man for our freedom, even if it would have taken us thirty more years. There would have been more deaths on both sides. . . . Morrison and the peace movement, I am convinced, helped to shorten the war, and therefore saved lives."

In a poem that he wrote while we were in Hanoi, Emily's partner, Clark, touched the heart of the painful paradox in Vietnam:

How Strange It Is

How strange it is
To ask the bird to hunt the tiger
Or launch a million souls to Death.

And stranger still
That the bird, when done,
Should return to song and nest.

We needed some light moments on this trip, or else we were in danger of drowning emotionally. Supper with Phuong's family was a relaxing contrast to all the formal dinners and meetings. And one evening, Hanoi's famous water puppets fascinated us with their traditional folk legends and themes at the Kim Dong Theatre. Emily was ill that night and couldn't attend, and when Thuy left the show early to check on her, he said that he was "holding her in the Light."

Finally diagnosed by a doctor, we found that Emily had been ill with the Asian flu since the second day of the trip. She was having trouble breathing and the full schedule was taxing for a pregnant woman. The care and concern our Vietnamese guides gave her and Norman's unborn grandchild were deeply appreciated and symbolic to her.

Fortunately, we all were able to make an excursion to beautiful Ha Long Bay, north of Hanoi. Out on the water, we all became quiet. We were deep in our own individual reflections and feelings as the little boat plied among a host of mysterious craggy islands and grottoes.

And it was nothing but pleasure to visit a women's coastal fishing project, an effort assisted by Quaker Service and managed by the local Women's Union. About three dozen women had bought into a communally owned fishing net. They were catching enough fish and shrimp not only to feed their families but also to make a small profit each day. The project, and others like it, encouraged entrepreneurship among rural Vietnamese women, who are often the sole supporters of their families.

Driving through the fishing village to the Gulf of Tonkin, we passed thatched-roof huts with walls of woven mats and earthen floors. The villagers, we learned, typically eat two meals each day, consisting of rice, fish, sauce, and sometimes a vegetable or two. When we reached the seaside, our van mired in the sand. Undaunted, we happily abandoned the van and our shoes, quickly merging with a group of fishing women and their children.

Looking joyful and industrious, the children were playing around the fishing gear and boats. Some of them were helping to cut up jellyfish to export to China. It was as much fun to photograph the children as it was daunting to try to help the strong women pull in their huge net from the sea. Theirs is a difficult and tenuous existence, dependent upon the catch of the day and threatened by typhoons, to which the coastal plain is frequently held hostage.

We returned to Hanoi and the long-awaited day when we were to meet To Huu, author of "Emily, My Child." The meeting took place in a spacious room in the office building of the Communist Party of Vietnam. From the moment we stepped from our van onto the long strip of red carpet that ran inside the building, the occasion felt formal.

The poet, short and stocky, with salt-and-pepper hair, stood and welcomed us with the good-natured confidence of one whose place in society is certain. His face often folded into a smile that almost closed his eyes. "Norman's sacrifice was not meaningless," he said. "We respect our national heroes in the same way as we respect Morrison."

To Huu said to us: "We consider each other as brother and sister. So rare! In such a world full of crimes, the two peoples of our country as brothers and sisters." And he added warmly: "You have made your way home. The Pacific cannot separate us. For you and for us, this is the *pacific*—the 'peaceful'—ocean. Now it is the friendship ocean."

I conveyed my deep gratitude to To Huu for his poem. "I didn't think I was writing the poem 'Emily, My Child,'" he replied. "I thought it was my heart, and the heart of the American people, writing it. I am going to be eighty now. I will never lose my confidence in the American people. . . . I hope you will keep the torch and flame of peace and justice in your hearts."

The poet continued, "Uncle Ho once said that Jesus Christ, Buddha, Confucius, and Lao-Tzu, if they sat together, would have been good friends because of their humanity." He told us that during the war, the Vietnamese people fought not only for their own thirty million citizens, but also for all three billion of the world's people. "We are poor in money, but we are rich in patriotism and our love for humanity and peace," he said. He wished our family health and happiness, and he expressed his hope that this would be only our first visit to Vietnam, with many more to come. "We have enough rice and bananas to welcome you!"

To Huu then reflected: "It's a happy day, because we are not thinking of death but of life and the future. I have known that Emily will become a mother. My congratulations to you. I hope it will be a beautiful child, and a wise and intelligent one. The child—he or she—will carry the blood of Morrison in his heart. That is an unbelievable happiness."

After our conversation over tea and coffee, the meeting turned into a poetry reading. Christina read "Peace Pagoda," and Clark recited "How Strange It Is." Jefferson read the following haikus he had written, inspired by the trip:

> *Morning bird awakens.*
> *Ha Noi gives rhythm.*
> *Rising, my heart keeps the beat.*
>
> *Cold wind, then hot sun.*
> *Soon the rain begins.*
> *Seasons claim the tools of war.*
>
> *Heroic battles,*
> *Stories of valor,*
> *Memories fade, spirit grows.*
>
> *Thank you, Viet Nam!*

The poems were translated on the spot, and they created much good feeling in the room. "You are all young Walt Whitmans!" To Huu exclaimed with a laugh.

It was especially moving in that context for me to hear Emily read the poem she had written to To Huu. Its words sank into my heart, creating a turbulent pool of feelings and memories. When I had first received a copy of "Emily, My Child," a few weeks after Norman's death, I could scarcely read it, I was so overwhelmed with emotion. Over the years, I have read it many times, never without a catch in my throat.

I thought that day of Emily's childhood years, when I did not share our family's story or the poem with her, always waiting for her to be "old enough" to hear it and bear the weight of it. I waited too long. I felt regret and embarrassment when she told me that Staughton Lynd, a family friend, had told her about the poem on a visit he made to George School while she was a student there. He subsequently mailed her a copy. When Emily told me, I also felt relief and joy that she had the poem at last.

All that emotion returned as I listened to Emily read her tribute to To Huu. Her poem—presented, it seemed, as to an elderly uncle—connected my heart's ache to the old ache in hers. I was grateful beyond words for it:

For To Huu

In Viet Nam,
In the dust and blood
Days after my father died,
You wrote a poem.
For many people
You created in words a symbol
Of hope and the future with
"Emily."
You helped those to understand
My father
And to love me from afar.

I did not know you wrote a poem.
In America I was a strange child
With an odd past,
Someone who did not like to tell the
Long story of her childhood
Or her father's death
When I was 15

A friend told me there was
A poem about me.
A week later he sent it to me.
I waited to open it
Until I was outside
Under a large fir tree,
On the grass,
Alone and safe.
As I read the words
I cried.
To someone and
Some country
I was not strange or odd.
I was a daughter
Left and loved,
Honored
And understood.

Thank you for giving me a
moment,
A feather
Under a tree
That helped me
Carry the weight of my past
More lightly and
Wholly.
Thank you for writing a poem
Wherein
The love my father felt
For a far-off land
Traveled back
And rested in my
Heart.

8

"Unless a Grain of Wheat Dies . . ."

Jesus gave himself—body, mind, and spirit—to the world and its problems, and he is asking us to do the same.
—NORMAN MORRISON

I had been wondering how I was going to get Pham Van Dong's beautiful gift of The Compassionate Buddha with a Thousand Hands—with its many tiny, delicate arms—home safely. It was almost two feet tall, resting in a velvet box without a handle. Ever the resourceful one, Phuong had come up with the solution: a rice sack. She placed the box in the large sack, tying a string-rope into a makeshift handle.

Our first test came at the Hanoi airport. As the rice-sack box was rolling through security, the young male clerk stared perplexedly into his x-ray camera. "What is it?" he asked.

"A Buddha," I replied.

"What did you say?"

"Buddha. The Buddha," I repeated, folding my hands and bowing.

"Ah, the Buddha!" the clerk smiled. "Go on, go on through."

Christina, Emily, Jefferson, Clark, and I were flying from Hanoi to Da Nang for our week in the South of Vietnam. I had always associated Da Nang with a military airfield, since Norman and I had a letter-writing friend who was based there during

140

the war. Da Nang is a city at the seventeenth parallel—the demarcation line that divided Vietnam into North and South, beginning in 1954 until reunification in 1975. There we boarded a minibus for the trip through Quang Ngai province. We were headed to My Lai.

Our friends at the Vietnam-American Society assigned us a new guide, Bui Van Nghi. It was hard to say goodbye to Thuy and An, of whom we had grown very fond. Twenty-nine-year-old Nghi was an open, friendly, and very young-looking fellow. He had recently studied at the City University of New York on Staten Island, where he had lived with an American Vietnam War veteran and his family.

En route to My Lai, we stayed overnight at a government guesthouse in Quang Ngai town, only a few blocks from the site of the American Friends Service Committee's wartime prosthesis center. Although I regard myself as someone used to "roughing it," I found the bed and pillows at the guesthouse incredibly hard. I was reminded that a typical Vietnamese peasant sleeps on a mat bed with a bundle of bamboo sticks for a pillow. At Christina's insistence, we requested bed linens.

About five o'clock in the morning, I was awakened by the sound of lively instrumental music. It seemed to be coming from a radio outside, nearby. There was something surreal about the music. Maybe it melded with a dream I was having. To the rhythm of the music, I heard a song very clearly in my head, over and over:

> *Who made the night?*
> *"It is I, it is I," saith the Lord.*
> *Who made the day?*
> *"It is I, it is I," saith the Lord.*

I got up and wrote in my journal: "Vietnam is God's world. It is holy, like my native land is holy. God is in charge here, and there. Leave the world alone; just do the work that only I can do. Lord, give me the strength to do it, to be fully present in the priceless moment of Now." That was my prayer that morning, as we set our sights on My Lai, the one place in Vietnam I knew I had to visit.

My Lai is a group of tiny rural hamlets that make up the village of Song Mai, near the South China Sea. For America, My Lai was surely our defining moment of darkness in the war. It was the place where, on the morning of March 16, 1968, U.S. soldiers massacred 504 unarmed Vietnamese civilians, mostly children and women. Platoon leader Lt. William Calley was court-martialed for his role in the mass slaughter, and later pardoned by President Richard Nixon.

The My Lai memorial—a commemorative park with a small museum, visitor center, garden, and monuments set among trees and shrubs—stands on the site of the massacre. The museum's walls are lined with photographs from that horrific event. The guide on the day that we visited was a beautiful, young woman wearing a white *ao dai*, the formal, elegant, mandarin-style shirt and trousers of Vietnamese women. She wept as she related the story of My Lai.

Early on the morning of the massacre, she said, the villagers were cooking their rice and going about their usual chores. At 5:30 a.m., machine-gun fire pummeled the village, reported to be a haven for Viet Cong soldiers. Then U.S. troops dropped to the ground from helicopters. For four hours, U.S. soldiers wounded and killed civilians, raped young women, burned huts, and contaminated wells with dead animals and human corpses.

But My Lai is also a place where human compassion and American honor were upheld through the heroic action of U.S. helicopter pilot Hugh Thompson and his crew, Larry Colburn and Glenn Andreotta, who were flying reconnaissance for the operation at My Lai that morning. Seeing first with disbelief, then horror, the carnage on the ground, an infuriated Thompson landed his helicopter close to a group of U.S. troops advancing toward a cluster of scared villagers huddled in a bunker. Colburn, the helicopter's gunner, held a machine gun on the troops while Thompson—ignoring orders and risking his career, if not his life—ushered the villagers to safety.

Their story was buried in the Pentagon for almost three decades. Just before the thirtieth anniversary of the massacre, the U.S. Army gave Hugh Thompson and Larry Colburn the Soldier's Medal for heroic action in a ceremony at the Vietnam War Memorial in Washington, D.C. Glenn Andreotta was awarded the medal posthumously. Thompson and Colburn returned to My Lai in March 2001 to participate in the dedication of a second Peace Park there.

We found My Lai, with its mass graves and monuments, to be a place of intense sadness, yet also peacefulness. It was a place where prayer seemed the most appropriate response. In the garden, people spoke in hushed tones or were silent. We wandered quietly, reading the markers designating where peasant huts had once stood and listing the names of those who had died there.

Dominating the park is a huge granite statue of a strong Vietnamese woman, holding protectively, Pieta-like, her slain companions. We took turns burning incense at the monument, pausing for a few moments to pray, meditate, or cry. Emily and I sat together under a tree, our arms around each other. I could have stayed there for a long time. How long, I wondered, will My Lai remain in the collective memories of our two countries?

After such an intense encounter with the past, it was a relief to experience life as it is now in Quang Ngai province. Tran Thi Ngoc Lan, president of the province's Women's Union, arranged our visit to a thriving shrimp farm. Under a hot, bright sun, we walked single file along narrow mud dikes that ended at a river's edge. As we watched a group of young children happily splashing and swimming, I thought again of Ben at that age and how he would have loved to swim and play with those boys in the river.

The proud shrimp farmer was a quiet and dignified man, middle aged and weather beaten. He told us that, in a good year, his extended family of seven makes an income equivalent to two thousand American dollars. The family graciously invited us to its nearby home, a comparatively spacious tropical hut of bamboo and reed mats. There we had our first experience of watching someone shinny up a palm tree, machete in hand, and bring down coconuts. We sat on plastic chairs and stools in the yard and drank fresh coconut milk. Several neighbors gathered with us. It was a relaxed and happy moment. Christina's comment, "I wish we could have stayed there all afternoon," expressed my own feelings.

But we were late for a visit at the elementary school, coordinated by Mike Boehm and Nguyen Duy Viet, with Phan Van Do as our generous and good-natured interpreter. At least a hundred students and their teachers—the entire school—were waiting for us in the hot schoolyard. As we drove up, the children shouted in unison, "Welcome to the Morrisons! Welcome to the Morrisons!" A couple of teachers stepped forward with a huge box of treats for us to give to the children. When Christina and Emily and I tried to distribute them, chaos reigned. The kids overwhelmed us with their excited pushing and jostling, and we finally gave up and asked the teachers to distribute the candy and cookies for us.

Inside the simple, open-air schoolhouse, we viewed a room filled with student art—an exchange project between students at My Lai and an elementary school in Madison, Wisconsin, sponsored by the Peace Park Project. The creative artwork of the Vietnamese children sparked in Christina the idea of developing a line of greeting cards from the drawings of the My Lai schoolchildren. The cards are now being distributed by the Madison Friends Meeting, with proceeds going to community-development projects in Vietnam.

In the bare earth of the schoolyard, we planted several trees and released a cage of "peace pigeons"—Vietnamese substitutes for doves. We had our pictures taken with the schoolchildren under their huge banner, which proclaimed, "Welcome to the Morrison Family from the My Lai School." As our minibus drove away, a few older children ran alongside us down the lane, as far as they could.

After the school visit, there was just enough time to get to a seafood luncheon on the shore of the Eastern Sea as guests of

Pham Huu Ton, the affable vice-chairman of Quang Ngai province, and some of his associates. The atmosphere was relaxed and jovial, and there were many toasts with Tiger Beer. The girls and I even had time to dip in the sea for a few delightful minutes.

For the most part, traveling in Vietnam was difficult and challenging. The air was sweltering and humid, and our minibuses were not air conditioned. That meant open windows, with dust and fumes rising up from the road. Most of the roads we traveled were in poor condition, part of the infrastructure of the country in much need of repair.

On the highways, as well as in towns and villages, virtually all the roads were clogged with people on foot, bikes, and motor scooters. Bicycles were often precariously laden with goods of all description. It was not uncommon to see a man carrying on his bike a chest of drawers, or several long pieces of metal pipe or wooden poles. Buses, minivans, trucks, and a few cars wove in and around the cyclists, constantly blowing their horns. There were many close calls, and one day we encountered what I was both dreading and expecting: a fatal accident, with a young man lying inert under a large truck and a crowd looking on helplessly.

Vietnam has a largely outdoor culture. People could be seen at work in the greening rice paddies, which stretched for miles along the roadways, or on the sidewalks drinking tea, cutting hair, mending bicycle tires, or cooking noodle soup. Houses often also serve as shops. Everywhere, families were in evidence, from toddlers to their grandmothers—and the ubiquitous motor-scooting youth. The majority of the country's population is young, largely due to the loss of so many adults in the war.

It took us several hours to get back to Da Nang. We arrived in time for a memorable dinner in our honor at a hotel, hosted by an affable group of leaders of Da Nang City, who reminded me of the executive committee of an American city council. They included Lam Quang Minh, the vice-chairman of VUS of Da Nang City; Le Thi Tam of the local Women's Union; and Nguyen Hoang Long, vice-chairman of the People's Committee of Da Nang City.

I sat next to Long, a friendly, gray-haired, and distinguished-looking gentleman. He told me he had "visited the Potomac and the Pentagon site where Morrison had died." He said he had wanted to find the spot for himself. After the war, Long had served on Vietnam's delegation to the United Nations. For a time, our government had quarantined the delegation to within twenty-five miles of New York City. Long spoke enthusiastically about an occasion when some Philadelphia Quakers persuaded U.S. government officials to allow the delegation to attend a Quaker picnic in their city. "We were so excited to be able to travel outside New York City," he said. "We made spring rolls to take to the picnic, and had a wonderful time."

In Da Nang, Emily was still ill, now with ear pain that likely signaled an infection. But, because of her pregnancy, no available medicine was safe for her to take. I requested an extra day in Da Nang so that she could rest. However, airline officials told Lady Borton that it was impossible to change our flight plans to Ho Chi Minh City. Grimly trying to make the best of a painful dilemma, we moved on—from hot to hotter.

The city formerly known as Saigon is more commercial and Americanized than Hanoi, with broader streets and more aggressive begging. It was heartbreaking to see so many children on the streets. We were warned against giving them money. I bought postcards from a few insistent ones.

One day, when Nghi, Lady, and I were sightseeing, we stopped by the old Rex Hotel, which has been handsomely refurbished by the government since the war. As Lady was checking her e-mail, a young travel clerk engaged in small talk with Nghi. It turned out that the two young fellows were from the same province and had attended the same high school. Out of the corner of my eye, I saw them looking at me, so I went over to say hello.

"I know your name!" the clerk said, beaming a smile. "Morrison! And I know the poem!"

"You're too young to know that poem or to remember the war," I teased.

He responded by boldly launching into "Emily, My Child," stumbling after a few lines. "But in school, when I recited it," he protested proudly, "I got a grade of eight out of ten!" At the end of our conversation, he smiled again and declared, "I can't wait to tell my mother and father that I met you!"

Although it was only midmorning when we met with Ho Chi Minh City's Writers and Artists Union, it was already stiflingly hot. The building in which we gathered was experiencing a power failure, so there was no air conditioning—not even a fan. But the oppressive heat didn't inhibit our camaraderie and the surprisingly intimate exchange of feelings and thoughts between us.

Despite the obvious cultural differences, we felt like colleagues in the artistic endeavor. Emily, who studied theater and film at New York University and is talented in poetry, photography, and literary and visual arts, works with developmentally disabled adults in the creative arts. Clark, who also writes poetry, is a Celtic musician as well as an artist with stone and wood, and a graphic designer. With a talent for painting, sculpture, and dance, Christina uses her healing touch through therapeutic massage. Jefferson helps schoolchildren learn through gardening and landscape design. Any talent I have lies in the written word. Unfortunately, on that day Christina was nursing a sore leg back at the hotel, so she and Jefferson missed a meeting at which they would have felt right at home.

Anh Duc, vice president of the artists' union, told us that Norman's sacrifice "contributed to our struggle for independence." Several years ago, Duc said, he too had visited the United States and gone to the place where Norman sacrificed himself in order to pay tribute to him. "Please be like a member of our family," he said. "We can talk together as family."

I expressed a few words of gratitude, which Emily echoed. "During the war," she said, "there was much that was said that was untrue. But many artists spoke from the heart and spoke the truth." Emily invited the Vietnamese artists to help her put together a documentary to honor the artistic expressions that were inspired by Norman's sacrifice. And she gave thanks that our last official meeting in Vietnam was with artists because, she said, recalling the gift of To Huu's poem, "my first experience of the Vietnamese people and their compassion and wisdom was through art."

During the war, Vien Phuong, poet and president of the Artists and Writers Union, was living in Cu Chi, an elaborate, 150–mile network of multilevel tunnels north of Ho Chi Minh City. The tunnels were dug over a ten-year period for protection and shelter for some sixteen thousand resistance fighters during the war against the French and then against the U.S.-supported South Vietnamese regime. Like many others, Phuong learned of Norman's sacrifice over the radio. "The flame that Morrison set was burning in our hearts," he said. "We thought, if a young man with a happy family sacrificed happiness for a noble cause, why couldn't we Vietnamese people sacrifice ourselves for our country?"

Anh Duc was working for the revolutionary radio operation in South Vietnam during the war. "We broadcast the news of Morrison's sacrifice," he said. "That's how people in the South knew about your family. We knew about the mass demonstrations in the United States, but Morrison's sacrifice was individual. The image of Morrison in front of the Pentagon seared our memories. We knew Morrison was a father. We could feel his sacrifice on behalf of all Vietnamese people. We were profoundly moved."

I had heard similar words from many people in Vietnam, but I was particularly touched by Anh Duc's account. Maybe it was the cumulative effect of many such sharings over two weeks. Perhaps it was the earnestness in Anh Duc's face. Or maybe I was finally, truly understanding how deeply and uniquely Norman's act affected the hearts and souls of the people of Vietnam.

Anh Duc wanted to know if Clark had known about Emily's father before he met her. "No, it's very different in America," Clark replied, aware during this trip that Norman was far better known in Vietnam than in his own country. And then Clark announced, "We have one more introduction." I caught Clark's grin and said proudly, "Emily is carrying a baby—Morrison's grandchild. Morrison's grandchild is visiting Vietnam right now." Great smiles of joy broke out all across the room at the news.

Throughout our meeting, Huynh Phuon Dong, a graphic artist with a large smile, was sketching us. His shirt was completely drenched with sweat when he presented individual portrait sketches to us with a look of proud satisfaction. After a group photograph, we reluctantly said goodbye to this company of friends.

Again, we needed a break from all the heartwarming, and heart-wrenching, war stories. A motorboat ride through the winding canals of the Mekong Delta ended at the shrimp farm of Thieu Thi Tao, and her husband, Anh Cong: Eco-Aquaculture Mangrove Park. In a spacious and pleasant thatched hut, we enjoyed a lunch of shrimp prepared eight different, delicious ways. Cong, a tall man who looked as if he were made of wire and leather, was retired after sixty-three years as a revolutionary fighter. He shared his war stories with Nghi after lunch, while I responded to a beckoning I couldn't resist from a hammock hanging on the porch, overlooking the canal. My head and heart were filled with dozens of images, impressions, and feelings. I needed to be quiet.

During the war, Tao and her younger sister, Thieu Thi Tan, were teenagers when they were imprisoned in the tiger cages in the South. Their mother, Ba Binh, was head of the Committee for Prisoners in the South. She was arrested seven times during the resistance, she said, and tortured. Past traumas and hardships, however, did not seem to have dimmed the spirits of these three attractive and bright-eyed women. One evening we had dinner with their extended family in Ba Binh's tiny apartment, above a crowded, busy marketplace in Ho Chi Minh City.

In the city, we met two other women activists, old-school revolutionary leaders Nguyen Binh Thanh and Ngoc Dzung. Binh Thanh began resistance activities against the French while she was a schoolgirl at the Madame Curie School in Saigon from 1948 to 1950. In the early 1960s, she was fighting against the

South Vietnamese government and then, ultimately, the United States. She served as a member of the Vietnamese delegation to the United Nations from 1985 to 1987.

Thanh recounted a moment during the war at an international peace conference in Sofia, Bulgaria, in 1968. A Vietnamese delegate sang "Emily, Con"—the poem "Emily, My Child" set to music. As she sang, Thanh said, tears streamed down the singer's face. "There was not a dry eye in the crowd," she reflected.

Thanh and Ngoc Dzung told us they had met with peace delegations around the world from the 1950s to the 1970s. Both women were talking almost with one voice. "We knew that there were peace and freedom-loving Americans, but the average Vietnamese did not. They associated only GIs, bombers, and helicopters with America. For the average Vietnamese people, Norman Morrison changed their perspective on Americans. His death put a face on the peaceful Americans."

The lives of all these brave women bore witness to the fact that women have long played important roles in the history of Vietnamese political life. At an intimate dinner put on by Ho Chi Minh City's Union of Friendship Organizations, we had learned from Duong Dinh Ba, our host, that mothers have a revered status in Vietnamese culture. Ba told us that the Vietnamese word for "country" is *dat-nuoc* (*dat*, "land"; *nuoc*, "water"). It is an evocative and accurate term. Except for a few rugged mountains, Vietnam is a low-lying, often flooded, rice-growing country. Symbolically, its wetness is feminine, according to Taoist principle. The country's natural bounty is maternal and nurturing.

Before leaving Ho Chi Minh City, we visited the War Remnants Museum. I took no delight in seeing the U.S. tank and helicopter on display in the yard of the museum. It was difficult to look at many of the exhibits depicting the horror and suffering of the war for the Vietnamese, and also the toll it took on our own troops.

However, two photographs at the museum particularly fascinated me. One was of an agent of the U.S. Office of Strategic Services (OSS), precursor to our CIA, giving hand-grenade instruction to a cadre of Ho Chi Minh's guerrillas in their jungle hideout in the spring of 1945. The OSS provided training and arms to Ho's basically peasant forces, the Viet Minh, in their fight against the Japanese army, which had invaded Vietnam in 1940 during World War II. In exchange, Ho Chi Minh provided intelligence information to the OSS.

The other photograph was of Ho Chi Minh in Hanoi on September 2, 1945, flanked by two U.S. Secret Service agents, declaring himself president of the Independent Democratic Republic of Vietnam. A great admirer of the U.S. Constitution, Ho had insisted on patterning Vietnam's declaration of independence after the U.S. declaration, inserting verbatim: "All men are created equal; they are endowed by their Creator with certain inalienable rights; among these are Life, Liberty, and the Pursuit of Happiness."

Peace in the new Republic of Vietnam, however, was tenuous and short-lived. By late 1946, France—which had been Vietnam's colonial ruler for seventy-five years—bombarded the port of Haiphong, killing several thousand civilians. In retaliation, the Viet Minh attacked French garrisons, and the French War was engaged. The United States financially supported the French in the war, as documents on exhibit in the museum testify. The war ended with the defeat of France at Dien Bien Phu in the summer of 1954, the first time that a Western nation was defeated by an indigenous Southeast Asian resistance movement.

After the war, the Geneva Accords, signed by the French and by Pham Van Dong for North Vietnam, temporarily divided the country into North and South and called for elections in 1956 to establish a national government for a unified Vietnam. Fearful that the resources and people of the country would fall under Ho Chi Minh's Communist control, the United States refused to sign the accords and inserted itself as the key outside power. We fostered the development of a pro-Western, non-Communist state in South Vietnam, initially under the former emperor, Bao Dai, and subsequently under the corrupt, authoritarian, and nepotistic Prime Minister Ngo Dinh Diem. Diem was assassinated during a coup in 1963.

The U.S. war in Vietnam claimed the lives of more than fifty-eight thousand of our soldiers. Estimates of Vietnamese deaths, which are difficult to verify, range from two to three million—many of them civilians. The long, tragic war finally ended on April 30, 1975, with Vietnam's determined resistance movement defeating the militarily superior United States. Vietnam is a country close to the earth, yielding like water; yet water is a force strong enough to erode stone.

I went to Vietnam curious and a bit apprehensive about what it would be like to travel in a Communist country. I came away with a strong sense that the main motivation of the average Vietnamese person during the war was independence from foreign domination and defense of native land rather than a deep commitment to Communist doctrine. Vietnam's extended-family social pattern and village culture may incline easily toward cooperative and communal ventures, yet we witnessed rigorous entrepreneurship on virtually every street corner and wayside in the North and the South.

Regarding freedom of information, state television was present on the airwaves—yet anyone with a satellite dish could tune into CNN, and copies of *USA Today* were readily available on city newsstands. While in Ho Chi Minh City, we heard that the city's TV station recently had aired *Unknown Images*, footage of the war shot by U.S. GIs and edited by French journalists.

I grew up with the belief that all Communist countries were de facto police states. In 1999, Vietnam seemed a far cry from a military state. Of course, we were VIPs on an agreed-upon agenda, but we experienced as much personal freedom of movement as we requested. In a span of two weeks of travel through cities, towns, and countryside, I saw only two armed guards; they were posted in front of the Ministry of Defense in Hanoi. In fact, I often wished for a traffic cop when I was trying to cross the impossibly congested streets of that city.

My last afternoon in Vietnam, Nghi, the young guide who had so valiantly steered us through our fatigue-laden second week, and I sat down together over beer and iced coffee at the Asian

Hotel. "Mrs. Anne," he began, "at your age, you could be my mother; I could be your son. So, I want to tell you some things."

Nghi reflected: "During the American War, every family in Vietnam was affected. We endured much suffering." Nghi told me that one of his uncles had come home on leave during the war and learned that his wife was pregnant with their first child. He did not want to go back to fight, and planned to desert. "My grandparents were ashamed," continued Nghi, "and said to him, 'Have you no courage? Remember Morrison, the sacrifice he made for us.' My uncle returned to the front and was killed. He never saw his only son. This hurt my family very much. I lost three uncles in the war. Nearly every Vietnamese family suffered similarly during that war."

After Nghi shared his family's sorrow, I had little to say and much to ponder. I asked him, "How have you been able to forgive us Americans, and the French, Japanese, and Chinese, who have caused such destruction to your land and people for so long?"

The question seemed to puzzle him. He tried to explain. "It's just in our nature," he answered. "We want to look ahead, not hold on to the past, not hold hedges." I smiled. He meant to say "grudges," but I think "hedges" wasn't a bad choice of word. Hedges are living walls that divide and isolate. "If you hold on to the past too tight," Nghi went on, "you miss the present and the future." As I left him, Nghi pressed a piece of paper into my hand.

I was amazed that throughout our Vietnam journey, we encountered little to no expressed resentment toward America or Americans. Instead, we consistently encountered openness, friendliness, and curiosity. When I asked our hosts in various places, "Why do the Vietnamese seem so forgiving of us?" I never received a direct answer. Like Nghi, they seemed baffled by the question.

When I had put the question to Giang, our young interpreter at the meeting with Pham Van Dong, he had replied, "We are a small country, and we have learned that we must get along with our neighbors. We have a tradition of burying the past and looking to the future."

Giang described the invasion of Vietnam by China many centuries ago, led by the son of the Chinese emperor. When the Vietnamese captured and killed the emperor's son, his troops fled back across the border, according to Giang. "Then, we wanted to make restitution," he said. "We had a bronze statue made of the emperor's son and sent it back to the emperor as a peace offering, a sign of respect and mourning."

Yet even in a country so apparently forgiving, vengeance can distort the spirit. When the American war ended in 1975, the new Socialist Republic of Vietnam established harshly repressive "reeducation" camps. Military officers, government workers, and others who had cooperated with the United States were punished with hard physical labor and indoctrination. Disease, lack of food, and dangerous work such as sweeping mine fields contributed to a high death rate in the camps. Clearly, it was difficult for those who had fought and suffered for independence and reunification to forgive those who had collaborated with the other side. When I asked Nghi about this, he looked down and said quietly, "Those were difficult times."

From what we observed, those difficult times are past. Vietnam appears to have grown more open and flexible, both politically and economically, in recent years. "We want to be friends to the world," we heard more than once. And the evidence is convincing.

I went to Vietnam not knowing what to expect of this land halfway around the world. I came away with a kaleidoscope of impressions. The overarching one—the one that stays with me most clearly—is the beauty of the Vietnamese people. I was moved by the combination of strength and tenderness we witnessed in the Vietnamese, how ready they were to speak to us from the heart, how wise and poetic and forgiving they were. Midway through our sojourn, Christina had remarked astutely, "In Vietnam, the women are strong, and the men are not ashamed to cry."

Each of us on this journey carried personal burdens and challenges, and each of us left with unforgettable experiences, our lives forever altered. I went to Vietnam to say thank you to the people for their kindness and love expressed to us so many years ago. I came away with more love than I knew was possible from strangers too numerous to count.

About a year before we traveled to Vietnam, it became clear within me that God wanted me to make this trip, that it was the right thing to do. And that God's mercy would protect and guide us. All this was true, far more than I could have imagined.

I have just one regret about our trip. I wish we had searched for the village of Duc Co, whose tragic story had so moved Norman at the end of his life. The village probably no longer exists, but I would have liked to stand where Father Currien's church once stood. Surely the road to Pleiku, along which the wounded priest had stumbled with the remnant of his congregation, is still there. I would have liked to walk on that road in honor of those whose deaths inspired Norman's.

The last face I remember seeing in Ho Chi Minh City was that of an old beggar, his cap outstretched, approaching our rolled-up taxi window. As I fumbled in my purse for some change, our taxi sped away. I wish I could have handed him ten thousand *dong*. I would have liked to wish him well.

In the airport, I hugged my dear family, who were going on to Thailand to spend a few days relaxing and resting. I said a fond goodbye to Lady Borton, who had labored so diligently before and during those two weeks, and who intuitively shared in both our pain and our joy.

Once I was on the plane alone and settled in my seat, I unfolded the sheet of Asian Hotel stationery that Nghi had pressed into my hand. The poem he had written was simple and direct. As I read his heartfelt words, I was moved to tears. In a way, Nghi's poem says it all:

When a Little Child

When a little child, I learned a poem.
I knew the name Norman Morrison,

A simple Quaker man with a great heart
Sacrificed himself for sake of peace
To save the lives of many Vietnamese
And his fellow-Americans.

Since then I knew two Americas, two
Americans.
One with aspiration for peace and humanities
One with a lust of war-monger.
I respect the people who love peace
and hate the war
Like most of my Vietnamese compatriots
Like my country fellow people,
Like all progressive people on earth.

These days I had a chance
To welcome you all visit Viet Nam
How wonderful, how happy we felt
When thinking of the fact that
The Morrisons come home (Viet Nam).
Please consider our country your home
As for it your loved one sacrificed.
He is immortal.
He lives forever in our heart.

When returning the USA
I want you to convey my love
And the affection of Vietnamese people
To the people who braved their lives
for peace.
To normal Americans,
To Vietnam veterans.
Please tell them to come or come back.
Now my country, Viet Nam, is at peace,
Where people are open and friendly,
Really ready to make friends with them.

Viet Nam needs more and more friends.
Viet Nam loves peace and understanding,
reconciliation and friendship.
Viet Nam needs reconstruction of the country
To bring her people to better life.

May God bless Vietnam.
May God bless America.
May God bless all families in Viet Nam and
USA.

As the plane lifted off and I headed home to my own beloved America, I was overtaken by a great sense of peace. Maybe we did finally bury Norman under those three trees on the Peace Park hill. He belongs now to Vietnam. I didn't purposefully write a eulogy for him, but perhaps that is what I was doing in my journal as the exquisitely beautiful land of Vietnam faded away from view:

It is over. "Unless a grain of wheat falls into the earth and dies, it remains alone; but if it dies, it bears much fruit. He who loves his life loses it, and he who hates his life in this world will keep it for eternal life. If any one serves me, he must follow me" (John 12:24–27).

Like the grain of wheat, Norman died, yielding a harvest of inspiration, humanity and love as well as suffering, pain and sorrow. Whatever else, I believe that he was trying to his utmost to be loyal to his Christ of the cross.

As for me, each time I am able to die a little to my ego, fears and possessiveness, there is a yield, a harvest. Because then I open myself to the greater possibilities of the universe, including the possibility that God can and will work through me. Lord, may it be so.

Epilogue

The Light Still Shines

*The light still shines in the darkness,
and the darkness has never
put it out.*
—John 1:5

Standing in a corner of my living room is a small mahogany
sideboard. It's the first piece of furniture Norman and I bought—
secondhand—when we moved to Charlotte to help launch the
Friends Meeting there in 1959. It is now my family altar, which
I created upon our return from Vietnam, in the style of the altars we found all across that gorgeous country. It holds pictures
of Norman and Ben, Mother and Dad, and my childhood nanny,
Louella, along with several objects special and sacred to me.

There's the della Robbia painting *Madonna and Child* I was
given when I was pregnant with Emily and a statue of Saint
Francis, a rosary made by an Anglican friend and a cross carved
of olive wood from the Middle East, a sandalwood figure of a
Hindu Shiva and a tiny ivory likeness of Gandhi. Standing in a
pose of blessing over this holy array is the elegant statue of The
Compassionate Buddha with a Thousand Hands, with its many
delicate outstretched arms, the gift from Pham Van Dong.

Virtually every Vietnamese family has a table or dresser on
which religious objects are placed, along with a flower vase, a
holder for incense, and photographs of deceased loved ones. Incense is burned in memory of, and respect for, those who have
passed on. On special days, such as a birthday or the anniversary

of a death, colorful flowers, fresh fruit, or a cup of tea or beer are also placed on the altar. Friends and family gather around to pay tribute and to remember the one who has gone.

When the ritual was explained to me, I thought, "What a healing tradition of memory and respect." A country that has suffered so much for nearly two thousand years, Vietnam may have something to teach us about dealing with death and loss, and surviving. And about forgiving.

The war that devastated Vietnam created havoc and cut a deep chasm in our nation as well, plaguing us with profound hurt and cynicism from which we haven't fully emerged or recovered. Is it not time to finish binding up the wounds we caused in waging that war, both at home and in Vietnam? We especially need to find ways to forgive, even if many of us will never forget our experiences of that tragic period. The path to healing requires forgiveness of ourselves, of others—including the leaders who deceived or betrayed us at the time—and even of those we labeled enemy. Forgiveness can be the balm that soothes, even cures, a wound.

Jesus' commandments to his followers to love one another, to love our neighbors as ourselves, to love even our enemies, are more relevant today than ever. In Jesus' day, the world was both limited in perspective and at the same time too vast to comprehend. Today's world is vast but also closely connected and interdependent, due to global trade and rapidly expanding technology. Now, especially in a nuclear and terror-ridden world, we need to take seriously the mandate of learning to live in peace. As Martin Luther King Jr. said so eloquently, "Together we must learn to live as brothers or together we will be forced to perish as fools."

To live in peace requires that we pursue the essential values of compassion, economic and political justice, global understanding, and environmental survival. The debacle in Vietnam should have taught us to follow this course. But three decades after the end of the war, I have to wonder, have we learned the lessons of Vietnam? Do our leaders understand the importance of telling the truth? Have we grasped the arrogance of unilateral power? Have we learned the danger of using morally unacceptable means to achieve seemingly good ends? Do we understand the toll it takes on both civilian populations and our own souls to wage wars of such devastating magnitude and indiscriminate aim?

Sadly, the foreign policy of our nation in recent times has often stood for the opposite of our true and essential values. Rather than following the path of respect, diplomacy, and collaboration, we have pursued the way of independence, arrogance, and gain. This posture has created alienation at home and angered much of the rest of the world.

Though in the Vietnam war we paid lip service to "winning the hearts and minds" of the Vietnamese people, we were woefully ignorant of their history and civilization, and we overlooked and abused their very humanity. As a result, they, and we, suffered grievously, and suffer still. Tragically, this kind of error born of hubris has been repeated in Iraq. Again largely ignorant of the complexities of another society and its history, and driven by our own political and economic agenda, we invaded Iraq, calling ourselves liberators. In fact, we have been disdained as conquerors and occupiers.

Norman gave his life in the hope that our nation would turn away from war and embrace the ways of peace. His sacrifice compelled me both to defend his action and to forgive him for it, as I had to forgive myself for the ways I had failed him. I shared the great anguish he felt about the war, and I respected his courage and commitment to try to stop it. But his action resulted in a traumatic loss that took a tremendous, incalculable toll on our family—and still does.

For a long time after Norman died, I didn't experience or express anger. But over the years, I discovered that feeling my anger was a crucial part of my healing. I learned that healing starts with recognizing and admitting pain: acknowledging past wounds, giving them shape and form. Digging up and reexperiencing buried pain is a difficult task, but a necessary one. If we run away from pain, or shut it off, it will remain under the surface as an aching sadness, erupting from time to time as an exploding anguish. If a wound is festering, it needs to be reopened to be healed. The pain, or fear, or hate, has to be acknowledged and given to God. Then grace comes like a balm, like holy ointment that can start the healing process.

If we can face our own pain courageously, we can help others by reaching out in compassion and in solidarity with theirs. When my emotional dike finally broke, and I opened myself to Christina and Emily and their pain, we found a deep solace in the company of one another.

When Emily was growing up, I believed that she had been too young on November 2, 1965, to retain a memory of what had happened to her. Emily regrets not having had the opportunity to know her father well, but says that "his writings as well as the words and open arms of all those who understood and honored him have let me look into his eyes and feel the fullness of his heart." As she has wrestled with the impact of his taking her as an infant to the Pentagon, she has come to believe that her presence helped bring home the tragedy of the war and that her survival was a sign of hope.

The mystery is still there, I suppose, as to what exactly happened on November 2 when Norman gave his life. What my mind's eye, or my body, remembers is feeling confused, an image of my father kissing me, setting me down, and then quickly pouring something on his head. I remember smoke, and people yelling, and someone holding me.

In forty-two years, no one who was there to witness it has come forward to tell me firsthand exactly what occurred. If any such persons are still alive, I would be glad to hear from them. But the difficulty one would have dousing himself and lighting a kitchen match while holding a one year old, as well as my perfect physical health following the incident, support the probability that I was set down first.

By involving me the way he did, I feel Norman was in-
trinsically asking the question, How would you feel if this
child were burned too? People condemned him for my
presence there when perhaps he wanted us to question this
horrifying possibility. Perhaps we are still struggling with
the fact that we are responsible, even if unwillingly, for
millions of people and thousands of children being burned
to death in war. We are still responsible for children hav-
ing to watch their families die in front of their eyes, and for
all the orphans of all of our own brothers and sisters, fa-
thers and mothers, and sons and daughters who have been
dying for us as good soldiers.

I believe I was there with Norman ultimately to be a
symbol of truth and hope, treasure and horror all together.
And I am fine with my role in it. I have had, and still have,
a great relationship with Norman's spirit. I feel that I know
him as a friend. I appreciate his unusual act of great love
and all those who have honored it.

As I have grown and thrived, my life has been full of sup-
port, love, and many great adventures. I am thankful for and
honor my mother's abundant love, grace, strength, and great
courage in her life and mind, and in writing this book.

I am grateful for my rewarding work with developmen-
tally disabled adults. I am thankful for my two beautiful
children, and that I, and they, can share so much time with
my mother and stepfather. I am so grateful to all the friends
and strangers who have reached out to our family, here, in
Vietnam, and in other countries—and particularly to all the
veterans who have understood that Norman wasn't trying
to make things worse, but better, for all of us, including his
grandchildren.

Over the years, in letters and interviews and journals, Christina has also reflected eloquently on the impact her father's sacrifice has had on her life. Like her sister's, her thoughtful words
give me joy and hope:

I was five when my father died. I have a few, precious memories of him, like holding his hand as we walked to school and laughing as he spun me around to Scottish reels. I remember riding in our VW van full of inner-city kids as he drove us all to a lush green park, a place the kids wouldn't otherwise get to visit. Once there, my favorite part was riding on his shoulders as we walked down beautiful flower-lined paths.

His presence in our house was energetic, purposeful, fun, and distracted. Like most kids, I always wished he was around more. After he died, life went on, but all the colors faded and our home was strangely sad and empty. I never stopped half-hoping that some day his car would appear in the driveway with him waving hello like always.

On the night of his death, lots of people suddenly appeared in our home. Then my mother strode out the door in her long coat, looking like a queen on a mission. She didn't say where she was going. I huddled on the couch with my brother, Ben, feeling alarmed and bewildered.

I don't remember how I felt when she told us in the morning—mostly shocked, I'm sure. A parent's death is hard enough, but when parents take their own life, for any reason, it cuts deeper. A farewell note would have helped fill the hole he left in our lives and would've become my most precious possession. His letter to Mom told her to explain his action to us; it didn't say to tell us he loved us.

In a way, my father sacrificed all five of us in pursuit of his mission. I wondered how the people of a distant country could be more important than us. As a little girl who wanted to feel special to her daddy, my heart was broken and so was Ben's. I wondered if he thought of us as he drove to Washington. He had great faith, and I think he believed that grace would fill the void he left in our lives. For many years it didn't seem to.

After his death we needed space and time to grieve, but we were inundated by other people's questions and concerns.

Among ourselves we hardly ever spoke about him or his death, much less cried. It was all too painful, so we thought. I never saw my mother cry, and I followed her example. Ironically, our feelings were so overwhelming that we tried in vain to put them on a shelf.

Not only did we miss him, but we were also left with the arduous task of explaining a death we hardly understood. I came to dread the question, "How did your father die?" When I answered, people often responded with shock or disapproval. I struggled to explain it in a way that honored him, while feeling unresolved about it myself. Sometimes I said he died in an accident because it was so much easier.

As hard as our childhood was after he died, it was also fun and magical. We had great summers at our grandma's home in Chautauqua, New York, and at our mountain cabin in North Carolina. We spent days flying kites in high meadows, sliding down waterfalls, running barefoot across the thunder bridge, or picking wild blueberries, and nights stargazing on the deck, attending concerts at the amphitheater, or reading stories around the fire. Our dog, Whitefoot, was a sweet and constant friend and companion. Even with the loss of our dad, I always felt we were very fortunate— until Ben got sick.

Ben and I were close in age and did almost everything together. Knowing him was like knowing my dad, in many ways. They were strong, brave, physically adept, and focused, yet both had a sensitive, deep, sweet, and silly side as well. Life with Ben was never boring; we were often outside playing on rope swings, riding bikes or sliding down a snowy hill. He was incredibly dexterous and self-motivated for his age. By fifteen, he'd rebuilt a VW "Bug" and made two tree houses, a bunk bed, a totem pole, and a huge model airplane. It was always fun going to his room to see his latest project. He was also a prolific artist, and we still enjoy his many paintings, sculptures, and woodblock prints.

On our last Christmas together, Ben gave me a beautiful wooden box he'd made without nails by carefully drilling holes for wooden pegs. He only had a few months to live, and I'm sure he didn't feel very well. Yet he spent hours alone in his workshop making gifts for everyone. That box is the one thing I've kept through umpteen moves over thirty-three years.

I believe my father's death was harder on Ben than anyone. Being a boy and knowing my dad longer, he felt the loss more keenly. Losing our father had made a strong, if silent, bond between us; I wish I'd asked Ben about his memories of him. When Ben became ill, maybe he was calling for help. Standing helplessly by while he died in a cancer ward was the saddest experience of my life and added to the deep well of grief inside me.

Somehow, I managed to make it through my teen years and even enjoy life. I had a few close friends; music took me beyond myself; and nature was a source of solace, adventure, and wonder. My mother's constant love and support gave me confidence, but eventually anxiety and despair became the backdrop of my life.

In my twenties, I developed an illness that made me slow down and ask for help. Fortunately, I found many therapies that helped me begin to release the frozen places inside. I realized that emotions don't just go away with time and that it's never too late to feel, express, and heal. This experience set me on a path of healing myself and others through bodywork.

One of the things I miss most about my dad was being held by him. One day he was there and the next he wasn't, and I never held his hand or felt his arms around me again. Over time, my loss became a gift. When I'm massaging someone and feel that person relax under my hands, I realize that we're all children longing to be touched and held.

My father loved me very much, and the farewell note I didn't receive from him is mine to write. He left without a *goodbye so I could learn to love myself more. His father died in a sudden and unresolved way as well. Perhaps he needed and in some way still needs my love as much as I needed his. We're all in this learning-to-express-love thing together.*

Going to Vietnam made a silver lining in our story. The people we met treated us like family and poured love and gratitude all over us. They gave us beautiful gifts, served us fantastic meals, and toured us all around their country. They called Emily and me "daughters of Vietnam." I felt deeply honored and appreciated for our family's sacrifice in a way that I never had been by our own culture.

As a child, the only thing that helped me understand my dad's death was being aware of the suffering in Vietnam. Kids there were losing even more than I'd lost: their parents, families, and whole villages. I felt a special bond with them. On our visit, I got to meet some of those children, now grown, who cried as they told us how much my father's sacrifice meant to them, that somebody in America—land of the enemy—cared about them. This was indescribably healing for me.

We also met lots of lovely, exuberant children and received some of their beautiful artwork. I was so glad to see many happy, healthy kids, although many live in poverty and are disabled from the effects of chemical warfare or from stepping on land mines. Seeing firsthand the beauty and suffering of the land and people in Vietnam helped me feel even more accepting of my father's death.

The most surprising thing was how important my sister Emily was to them. Because of the poem "Emily, My Child," they couldn't wait to meet Emily, who had captured their hearts and imaginations. When I first learned that my father took my sister with him to the Pentagon, I found it unacceptable. Now I perceive it as a mystery and a miracle. Emily symbolized all the children who suffered or lost parents in the war, and who would live on, hopefully, beyond all wars. Amazingly, she was physically unharmed and, through To Huu's poem, her presence turned my father's message into a legend of love and hope that is an important part of Vietnamese culture.

My husband's father died serving in the war, and the Vietnamese welcomed Jefferson with great respect and kindness as well. In fact, they were fascinated to meet him and hear his father's story. They seemed to hold no resentment toward veterans; they hold only our leaders responsible for the war, and forgive even them. To feel their acceptance and forgiveness was an important part of my husband's acceptance of his father's death, his role in the war, and the war itself.

Few Americans would support a modern-day war if they directly witnessed the horror of it. My father showed the truth of what was happening. He was also hoping to give his life greater meaning and purpose. Yet, mostly, he wanted to express compassion for the Vietnamese, which is why his message touched them in such a powerful way.

My father was very passionate and felt a deep connection with all beings. It was hard for him to express his feelings, which led to their expression in an intense way. His act was a bittersweet paradox, a harsh one that came from and caused great pain, and a generous one of great faith and love. Trying to analyze his death or to make a final decision about it seems impossible. Yet it's certain that, as I said as a child, his love spread all over the world, including over me.

With a death like that, it's easy for the death to eclipse or define the life. Yet my father's life was filled with daring escapades, good work, spontaneous adventures, and many moments of humor and kindness. I'm proud of who he was and the way he lived, and I am grateful to my mother for writing this book so more people can know him better.

My father and brother are still very much with me. Planting lilies, walking down the trail, or dancing to music, I feel

*their spirits coming through. Memories of them stand out
in bright relief, more precious because of their passing. And
I enjoy and appreciate each person in my life more, knowing how fragile and fleeting we are. All is intertwined and
every act, small or large, has a ripple effect far greater than
we know. Each day is a challenge and an opportunity for
me to be the peace that my father sought and to see the
beauty that my brother loved in the world.*

Healing has come little by little, bit by bit. It is still going on.
I think the process may never completely end. For a number of
years, I tried to establish a life independent of my identity as the
widow of Norman Morrison. But more and more, I have come
to accept my life as it was and is, as something that happened
to me, for reasons and purposes beyond my knowing. I can look
now on all that happened with understanding and forgiveness,
with compassion and acceptance.

Ever since 1965, as November 2 approaches each year, I find
myself reflecting on what Norman's self-sacrifice meant to me,
to our family, and to others far and near. Over the years, these
remembrances have been experiences of both sadness and cher-
ishing. Often I have gone over in my mind our last day together:
sharing French onion soup, our lunchtime conversation,
Norman's piercing questions about how to stop the war and
what I would do if I ever lost him.

On November 2, 1991, All Souls' Day, my husband, Bob, and
I took a walk on the beach before sunrise under a bright crescent
moon. Then I sat on the porch of our home at Emerald Isle, on
North Carolina's Outer Banks, watching the waves roll in and
the sky grow from mauve to rose to blue. Thinking about
Norman and our family, I wrote in my journal:

*Norman, now and then and today especially, I feel your
gentle presence close by, blessing me, glad for me and for
my life. I know you have shared our individual pains, and
that you loved us as much as you could in life. After your
death, you still love us, perhaps even more. And we loved*

you as much as we could and we still love you. And all is forgiven, all around.

As the years have progressed, my peace about Norman has increased and my images of him have grown more joyful. On October 25, 1993, I wrote:

Somehow I feel that Norman still longs for my complete forgiveness. Finally, after all these years, I am more able to face the past, to face Norman again, and to forgive him, and to be forgiven for the ways in which I hurt him, too. Now, more and more, when I think of Norman I see a happy smile on his face, and once again, a twinkle in his blue-gray eyes. We can dance together again, he and I!

On May 19, 1995, as I was beginning to write this book, I reflected:

Over and over recently, I am feeling like an instrument in God's hands. I feel led to be where I am. It seems like my whole life has been taking me to this present moment, when I can witness to the love and guidance of the Divine, which is ever present in life, even if interwoven with violence and tragedy.

My prayer is for strength, greater strength than I have, to be able to write the book that needs to be shared with others. My strength and guidance will come from God and his angels, that I know. I only want to be faithful to truth and the highest within me and in the universe.

At times in the past few weeks, I have felt the presence of Norman beside me. It is not sad or solemn; rather, it has some amount of gaiety and happiness. His spirit is encouraging me. As always, he has faith in me; and I will try to not let him down in the writing of his life story.

Although I believe Norman intended his sacrifice to appeal in the strongest way to Lyndon Johnson, Robert McNamara, and the American conscience, it is clear to me now that his action spoke most profoundly (and probably unintentionally) to the Vietnamese people. Norman and Emily became part of their story, their inspiration, their history, their hope. Christina echoed my own sentiments when she said on our trip, "I'm very glad, if Norman had to send a special message of love and compassion to any people, that it was the Vietnamese. They truly deserve it."

What Norman did more than forty years ago in a desperate attempt to stop the war still shines brightly in the hearts of the Vietnamese people. In that sense, the fire he lit has never gone out. A few days after my return from Vietnam, I received an e-mail message from Nguyen Ngoc Hung, the professor who had spoken with such strong emotion at the Peace Park near Hanoi early in our visit. He wrote: "You have a large family here in Vietnam. The Vietnamese will forever honor and respect what Norman has done for peace in this land. Mother Earth in Vietnam has taken him in, and we will teach our children how to act honorably and bravely for Peace on earth!"

Since my return, I have spoken to many groups about my Vietnam trip and my life's journey. Sometimes after I have shared my story, someone will ask: In the end, was Norman's sacrifice right or wrong? Is taking one's own life ever justified? When I consider the suffering our family has endured, to the second question I would have to answer no.

But in the larger scheme of things, I cannot say no. After looking into the eyes of the Vietnamese people, hearing their stories, and learning about the message of universal love that Norman's action conveyed to their hearts, I realize that out of the ashes of agony and loss rose something profound. Because Norman's death, terrible as it was, was an act of love and courage, it conveyed unspeakable beauty and truth.

I usually end my talks by reading Nghi's poem—the one written on the piece of Asian Hotel stationery that I had unfolded on my flight home, which invites Americans to visit Vietnam and ends with a blessing on all Vietnamese and American families.

Copies of it have been shared with veterans suffering from post-traumatic stress syndrome and at a traveling replica of the Vietnam War Memorial. The greeting cards that Christina created from the pictures drawn by Vietnamese children have been included with words of hope in care packages sent to U.S. soldiers fighting in Iraq. So the blessings continue. Praise God, the wounds of that painful, wrenching war are slowly being healed.

Seven months after our return from Vietnam, at 11:30 p.m. on October 20, 1999, Jesse Liam Morrison Chapin came into the world, struggling all the way. Emily began labor in earnest around 10 o'clock that morning. She worked valiantly all day to deliver the baby at home, until complications compelled the midwives to rush her to the hospital. Jesse's head had to be turned before delivery, and it appeared with the umbilical cord wrapped around it. Congested with excretion in his lungs and stomach, Jesse couldn't breathe. The medical staff immediately whisked him away and began suctioning, administering oxygen and antibiotics. Thankfully, Jesse—a big, nine-and-a-half-pound baby—responded quickly. The staff kept remarking on his "resilient spirit."

I was a doting grandmother over this precious, beautiful boy. I was full of thankfulness and praise for God the Giver of Life, for Emily's great strength and courage, for little Jesse's special spirit, and for the unseen angelic spirits that hovered close through it all. It gave me great comfort and joy to know that the spirit of Jesse's grandfather, Norman Morrison, was thrilled with the birth of this strong little boy. I picture a Scottish reel being danced in heaven that night.

Among those with whom I shared the good news of the birth were our friends in Vietnam. They sent warm congratulations. Soon after Jesse's arrival, I wrote these words in my journal:

Now I am in the evening of my life. Looking back, I consider myself to be very fortunate. I have been privileged to work for peace and justice, to do social work, be a journalist, and to be a wife, mother, and now a grandmother. I have been enormously sustained by the love of family and friends, by God's grace, by nature, by morning quiet, by spiritual readings and silent worship in Friends meeting, and by writing. For the remainder of my life, I want to work on dying to ego. I want to experience more courage. I want to be able to say, "When I am old, I will be fearless."

A few years ago, on a visit to London, I saw the play *Mother Courage and Her Children*, by Bertolt Brecht. In the play, through the hardened, cynical eyes of Mother Courage, the underbelly of war is exposed: the greed and corruption that often lie beneath the honor, glory, and idealism. Mother Courage survived the Thirty Years' War—a needless conflict that decimated vast regions of Europe in the seventeenth century—but it claimed her three children one by one. Worn down by her grief, she finally fell into silence.

To me, the real heroine of the play is Katrin, the childlike, mute daughter of Mother Courage, who climbs on a rooftop and beats a drum to warn people of the oncoming army. Katrin knows she will be killed for her bold act, but she has a great heart. Her compassion is her gift, and she gives it away to save her village.

Like Katrin, like Jesus, some are called to make the ultimate sacrifice of their life so that others may live. Parents sometimes do this. Soldiers often do this, and we honor and applaud them. Norman Morrison gave his life to try to stop the war in Vietnam. With his heart, his soul, and ultimately his body, he gave his utmost for peace.

Thankfully, we are not all called to make the ultimate sacrifice. But I believe we are all called to live in such a way as to share our gift of life with others. What will we do with our gift? Where will we stand? For what, and with whom, will we stand in solidarity and compassion?

Not long ago I made a visit to Chautauqua and walked down its tree-lined streets once more. I recalled that the summer after

Norman's death, our family did not go back to the family cottage as we had other summers; the pain and loss were still too fresh. Sadly, some years later, Hazel sold the cottage. On my first visit after it was sold, I found myself drawn to revisit it.

The new owner welcomed me and graciously allowed me to wander from room to room. She had made many renovations to the interior, with bright paint and charming design, but it was still the cottage we had loved all those years. And, amazingly, she had left unpainted the doorjamb where Hazel had recorded her sons' heights, year after year. For a long while, I couldn't stop weeping in that place.

I still wish we had the old cottage to go back to. For so many years it was the one constant space in the hectic, uncertain life of our little family. But now I am able to return to Chautauqua without too much sadness. Just some sweet, poignant memories, and deep appreciation for what it meant to Norman to grow up there, and what it has meant for our family. I look forward to sharing Chautauqua in the fullness of time with Jesse, now eight years old, and his dear younger brother, Everett, who is five, as they grow up and make visits to that special place that so deeply shaped their grandfather. I hope they will come to know him through his spirit that lingers there.

Although keeping the cottage was not meant to be, Chautauqua was meant to be, I am convinced. One can always ask, what if? What if Jane Lee, my Duke classmate, had not written that unexpected letter to me in the summer of 1954, suggesting that I come up and work at one of the hotels at Chautauqua, a place I had never heard of? What if I had not accepted and made my long, uncertain way north in the summer of 1955, to that mysterious mecca in the western corner of New York state? But I did. I got off the bus, suitcase in hand, and walked onto the Chautauqua grounds, down the brick walk, and into my future life. Yes, I believe it was meant to be.

How amazing life is, how permeated with mysteries, great and small. To this day, I cannot eat French onion soup. It tastes too much like loss. But I have cultivated a deepened appreciation for mangoes. To my delight, we ate them in Vietnam at almost every meal, cut open in a particular way that I have since adopted. Mangoes taste like hope.

The mantra I held close in Vietnam, written by Julia Cameron, remains true for me: "Within me, I carry God. Within God, I am carried." In moments of grief and joy, in seasons of doubt and faith—through it all—I have felt carried by the Divine. This truth is a great and marvelous mystery.

Within this mystery, how are we to live? How else but simply to be who we are at our deepest core? To try to do our best—the best and highest we know—with the help of God, the Light within us. To act with humility and compassion, not knowing what will follow, surrendering any illusions of personal control over the outcome and consequences. To act with faith and trust, and leave the rest to God.

When I go to my family altar, I think of my last conversation in Vietnam with Nghi. He had explained to me the significance of the rituals of memory at Vietnamese family altars, the telling of stories and leaving of gifts on special days to honor lost loved ones: "This way, we feel we haven't really lost so much. Physically, our loved ones are no longer with us. But spiritually, they are still present, to give us love, encouragement, and advice. Sometimes we even argue with them! We believe they are nearby and know what and how we are doing."

Yes, if we truly seek it, each of us will find our own place to stand. And we can find comfort and courage in knowing that we never stand alone. Others, seen and unseen, are standing all around us, cheering us on.

Notes

Epigraph   Psalm 122, in Stephen Mitchell, *A Book of Psalms: Selected and Adapted from the Hebrew* (New York: Harper Perennial, 1994), 68.

Introduction: To Shine a Light

xi   Barry Lopez, "Flight from Berlin," in *Resistance* (New York: Alfred A. Knopf, 2004), 162.

xii   Albert Camus, "Return to Tipasa," in *The Myth of Sisyphus and Other Essays*, trans. Justin O'Brien (New York: Vintage International Edition/Random House, 1991), 202.

2: Relying on "Guided Drift"

9   "According to one historian . . . " David H. Fischer, *Albion's Seed* (New York: Oxford University Press, 1989), 699.

16   Gerard Manley Hopkins, "God's Grandeur," in *A Selection of His Poems and Prose*, ed. W. H. Gardner (London: Penguin Books Ltd., 1953), 27.

31-32   Carl Jung, *Memories, Dreams, Reflections* (New York: Vintage Books/Random House, 1963), 356.

3: "Now His Love Has Spread All Over the World"

36   Jean Larteguy, "A Priest Tells How Our Bombers Razed His Church and Killed His People," in *Paris Match,* October 2, 1965, reprinted in *I .F. Stone's Weekly,* November 1, 1965.

42   Fischer, *Albion's Seed,* 590-91.

45   Robin Frames, Column/Forum, Religion Section, *The Baltimore Evening Sun,* November 6, 1965. Loudon Wainwright, "The View from Here," *Life,* November 8, 1965, 34.

46   Letter from Dr. Marian Manly, in Paul Hendrickson, *The Living and the Dead: Robert McNamara and Five Lives of a Lost War* (New York: Alfred A. Knopf, 1996), 202

53-54   T. S. Eliot, "Murder in the Cathedral," in *The Complete Poems and Plays, 1909-1950* (New York: Harcourt, Brace and Co., 1952), 211-12.

55   Roger LaPorte, quoted in the *New York Times*, November 10, 1965; Alice Herz, quoted in the *New York Times,* March 17, 1965.

57   Abraham Heschel, quoted in Taylor Branch, *At Canaan's Edge: America in the King Years, 1965-68* (New York: Simon and Schuster, 2006), 358.

58-59   Thich Nhat Hanh, from a letter to Rev. Dr. Martin Luther King, Jr., June 1965, in "In Search of the Enemy of Man," in *Lotus in a Sea of Fire* (New York: Hill and Wang, 1967), Appendix, 105-7.

59-60   *Oedipus at Colonus,* an English version by Robert Fitzgerald, in Sophocles, *The Oedipus Cycle,* an English version, trans. Fitts and Fitzgerald (New York: Harcourt, Brace and World, 1949), 112, 160–70.

4: "Courage"
70   Rainer Maria Rilke, *Letters to a Young Poet,* rev. ed., trans. M. D. Herter Norton (New York: W. W. Norton, 1954), 59.

5: Lighting the Horizon
82   Brian Willson quotation, www.brianwillson.com/bio.

83-84   "The flame which burned you . . . " Brian Willson, *On Third World Legs: An Autobiography* (Chicago: Charles H. Kerr Publishing Co., 1992), 19-20.

85-86   "Norman Morrison" by Adrian Mitchell. Reprinted with permission of the author.

87-92   Hugh Ogden, "Chautauqua," reprinted with permission of *Friends Journal.*

92-93   George Starbuck, "Of Late," in *From Both Sides Now: The Poetry of the Vietnam War and Its Aftermath,* ed. Philip Mahony (New York: Scribner, 1998), 53. Used with permission.

93-94   Alexander Laing, "Norman R. Morrison, 1934-1965," reprinted with permission of *The Dartmouth.*

94-95   Dorothy J. Mock, "Journey of Love and Entreaty," *Friends Journal* (Philadelphia), November 2005, 17. Reprinted with permission of *Friends Journal.*

95-96   Robert McNamara, *In Retrospect: The Tragedy and Lessons of Vietnam* (New York: Random House, 1995), 216.

102-5   "Emily, My Child" by To Huu, published by the Vietnam News Agency in *The Vietnam Courier,* November 6-10, 1965. Reprinted with permission.

6: "The Bright Living Torch of Uncle Morrison"
111-12 Harrison Salisbury, *Behind the Lines—Hanoi* (New York: Bantam Books, 1967), 7.
115   Julia Cameron, *Blessings: Prayers and Declarations for a Heartful Life* (New York: Tarcher, 1998), 80.
119   Ho Chi Minh, "On the Road," from *The Prison Diary of Ho Chi Minh*, trans. Aileen Palmer (New York: Bantam Books/Random House, 1971), 34.

8: "Unless a Grain of Wheat Dies . . . "
155-57 Bui Van Nghi, "When a Little Child," reprinted with permission.

Epilogue: The Light Still Shines
159   Martin Luther King, Jr., from "The World House" speech, *Where Do We Go From Here?* (Boston: Beacon Press, 1968).